BETWEEN THE MOUNTAIN AND THE SEA

Memories of a childhood on Tristan da Cunha, the world's loneliest inhabited island

Gill Kimber

with Mike Bell

For all my family

May the adventurous spirit of our parents, Philip and Dilys Bell, live on in us!

INTRODUCTION

Our family spent the five years of 1956-61 on Tristan da Cunha, known as the world's loneliest inhabited island, where my father was chaplain with the Society for the Propagation of the Gospel (SPG). Altogether, there were about three hundred islanders on Tristan in those days, around eighty of whom were children. They shared only seven surnames. The original islanders had been sailors, who had called at the uninhabited island for fresh water, fish, seals and penguins, and had decided to stay. Corporal William Glass with his wife Maria and two children had settled in 1817 with a handful of other men. They called themselves 'the Firm' and signed an agreement in communal living, where everything would be equally shared, and nobody would have more status than any other. This ethic of fair shares and egalitarian self-government survives on the island to this day, especially important when everyone depends on their friends in the dangerous work of deep-sea fishing, their main source of income.

The foundation of the community developed when, in 1826, William Glass was joined by bachelor Thomas Swain from Hastings in Sussex, which brought the number of bachelors up to five, as other men had joined William. This state of affairs led the men to ask the captain of a passing ship, on its way to the island of St Helena, to see if any of the single girls there would be willing to come to Tristan to be married. Amazingly, some of the women agreed, and went back to Tristan on the same ship, to land and line up on the beach. Thomas Swain had vowed to marry the first woman who stepped ashore, and did so. The other men took their pick.

In 1835 Dutchman Pieter Groen (now called Green) was shipwrecked on the island, and he was followed by American whalers Thomas Rogers and Captain Andrew Hagan. In 1892 the barque Italia caught fire, but managed to beach safely in Seal Bay on the island, and Andrea Repetto and Gaetano Lavarello from Camogli in Italy decided to stay and join the small community. Italian descendants with the same surname still visit the island, where the hospital is named after Camogli.

The year we left Tristan, 1961, was the year when the so-called 'extinct' volcano erupted laterally at one end of the plateau, and all the islanders were evacuated to England. They stayed about two years, when most elected to return to their island home, once it had been pronounced safe to do so.

Island life has changed enormously since then. The volcano covered Big Beach and the canning factory, and so a small harbour was built to make loading and unloading easier. There are tarred roads where there were none before, cars and modern conveniences, and much easier traffic for islanders between Tristan and other countries. The fame of Tristan rock lobster (called 'crawfish' on the island), which flourish in its pristine seas, has

6

now spread globally. The island exports it to different countries, where it can be served in Michelin-starred restaurants. The main income and diet of the islanders is still generated from fishing and the export of fish to South Africa, and daily life is still physically very demanding. The ongoing work in the potato Patches, and the care of sheep and cattle, can involve a thirty-mile round trip on foot over Tristan's mountain.

It is still only possible to reach Tristan by going to Capetown in South Africa, and getting a berth on one of the few ships which ply regularly between Capetown and Tristan. The unpredictable South Atlantic weather continues to hold sway over island activities, and over the loading and unloading of ships and the visits of passengers.

Up to date information about Tristan can be found on the island website, https://www.tristandc.com

Table of Contents

"Memory is like a chain. We reach back into the past by a succession of links. I have kept alive little pictures of my childhood by repeatedly recalling them. Like having a copy of an ancient manuscript - I have an early copy, but the original is lost." C.R.Milne

Prologue

Island of Tristan da Cunha, South Atlantic
Thursday, 2 March 1961, 5.30am

The four of us had been waiting for ages on our wooden veranda, dressed in our boots, windjammers and sou'westers, so we saw it first. We ran inside shouting 'Daddy! Mummy! Fardy Sidney is here with the bullock-cart!'

My parents looked deathly tired. On Sunday, four days previously, the *RSS Shackleton* had radioed that she was arriving a month early, so we had to be ready to leave for Cape Town by 6.30am on Thursday. Only four days to pack for a family of six, after a stay of five years. All week my mother and Harriet, who looked after us all, had been washing and ironing and sorting. We had been helping too, emptying drawers, cleaning, making choices about our toys and piles of our things. My father packed them methodically into tea chests. He looked white and exhausted. He and my mother had averaged four hours' sleep a night since Sunday, and he had not gone to bed at all last night.

But we were ready. Our worldly goods were in those wooden boxes banded with metal. My brother Mike and I had used black paint and a stencil to write our surname BELL and destination SOUTHAMPTON, ENGLAND on each one.

'Go outside, children. It's your last chance. Keep out of the men's way,' said my mother. I grabbed my three-year-old brother Christy by the hand, and met Fardy Sidney and the others coming in through the front gate. Sidney was Christy's godfather or Fardy, and was the nearest thing we had to an uncle on the island.

He grinned at us, his teeth white in his weather-beaten face, took hold of Christy and swung him in the air. 'Where's you gwin, my l'il boy?' he said. Christy made a grab at his cap but Sidney dodged. 'I'se gwin on a ship!' said Christy, and Sidney put

10

him down and chucked him under the chin. Then he and the other men lifted the tea chests as if they weighed nothing, and began to carry them to the waiting carts.

We went outside the gate. Our house was at the head of a little green valley which ran straight down to the cliff edge. Beyond, in our sight every day for five years, was the South Atlantic Ocean in all its moods. Today sea and sky were grey in the pre-dawn. How many times had we run the length of the valley to where the cliff face was broken down and we could climb easily on to Garden Gate beach? We had taken it for granted, and now there was no time left.

We knew the black oxen yoked to the painted cart were not aggressive and were well under control. Even so, we tended to give them and their pointed horns a wide berth. They had been driven down the side of our valley to the flat at the bottom, and stood waiting patiently while our tea chests were going into the first cart.

We climbed up the valley side and ran to the ship rock, a big dark boulder with a flat top like a deck. We climbed on to its smooth back and hauled up Christy, then we sat down with our legs hanging over the edge as we looked out to sea.

The sun had still not risen. We'd been woken and bundled out of our beds very early, made to dress quickly and have a scrappy breakfast. There wasn't time to do things properly on such an exciting day. In the dim light we could just make out the grey frigate RRS *Shackleton* riding at anchor, which would take us to Cape Town in South Africa. There was no bay on the Tristan plateau and no port. We would be rowed out to the waiting ship in the island longboats, standing ready on Big Beach. Not long now.

'I love the *Shackleton*,' Lizzie remarked, kicking her heels against the rock.

'We had a lovely time coming back on it to our island,' I reminisced. 'That was two years ago and you were only five.' At twelve I was the eldest of the four of us and used to looking after everyone.

'I 'member the sailors made me a swing on the deck,' she added.

'I want a swing,' announced Christy.

'I can see the rope ladder going up the side of the ship,' said my other brother Mike, who would soon be ten.

'So can I,' asserted Lizzie, who usually agreed with him.

'Rubbish,' I said scornfully. 'Course you can't. It's still too dark.'

Mike and I argued about it a bit, and as usual neither of us would give in. After a while we slid off the rock and went back to the house where we found our parents with their macs and boots on, shutting the front door. The ox-carts were piled with our belongings.

'Come on children,' said my mother. 'It's time to say goodbye.'

Harriet was crying. She hugged us tightly, and picked up Christy and held him against her wet face, covering him with kisses. She was his Muddish, one of his godmothers, and had looked after him constantly since he had been born on the island three years ago. She clung to my parents and they had to disengage themselves gently.

12

'Be a good girl now,' said my father. 'We'll write to you.' Still weeping, she tied her headscarf round her head and prepared to go with us to Big Beach.

'Do you want to say goodbye to the house?' my mother asked us.

I didn't see much point. My bedroom, with its pink walls and board floor, had nothing of mine left in it. The bungalow didn't feel like our home any more. It was like the shell left when one of our chicks had hatched. We were leaving it behind for our next adventure and we loved being at sea. When we reached Capetown we would transfer to the Stirling Castle and voyage on to England.

But I had caught a strangled sound in my mother's voice and by now I was more attuned to her moods. I looked closely at her and saw her hazel eyes were filled with tears. My father put his arm round her and I realised they were both upset. It hadn't occurred to me that they might mind about leaving.

Sidney and the others flicked their whips and the oxen moved off slowly, needing encouragement up the other side of the valley. We started by following them, but they moved so slowly and we were impatient. Sometimes we ran ahead, sometimes back over the stony turf littered with cattle and sheep dung. We reached the biggest stream, the Big Watron, and the four of us clumped over the plank bridge while the carts lumbered slowly through the water and up the next valley side. Because we had boots on we turned round and splashed back through the water of the watron and then over the bridge again, our soles leaving wet patterned footprints.

As we went, we were joined by more and more islanders coming down from the village to see us off. Granny Mary caught up with us, her headscarf over her grey hair in its usual bun, her tanned face smiling through tears. She was Christy's Muddish too. Muddish Martha was with her and all the kids from school. My best friend Minnie came up to me.

'Hish y'all gwing away for hever?'

'Yes we iss,' I said.

'Hi wish you didn't.'

'We'se got to,' I said matter-of-factly. We children knew that our time on the island was up, and we were returning to England for good.

1. IT ALL BEGINS

October 1955. Downham, near Bromley, Kent

I remember the first time Mummy told me I had to come home from school on the bus on my own. I was six then. I was scared and started to cry because I didn't know how to do it. She put on her no-nonsense-now voice and she explained exactly. I needed a penny in my hand. I was to get on the bus carefully – no running and jumping on the platform - and sit down. The conductor would come round with his leather money pouch and his ticket machine slung round his neck. I was to say 'penny please' and give it to him. He would wind the handle on his machine and give me my ticket. And here was the bus stop to get on, and here was the one to get off. After all, I'd been on the bus lots of times with her. I would soon get used to it.

And I did. The first time, I forgot to get my money ready before I left school. My cheeks felt hot while I stood in the queue at the bus stop because I had to hunt in my navy knicker-pocket in front of everyone for the penny, but I didn't make that mistake again. Now, a year later, at the age of seven, in class two at St John's Primary School with nice Miss Rowe instead of horrible Mrs Powell, I was an old hand.

That October afternoon I got off the bus at the usual stop. St Barnabas' Parsonage was built on its own triangular piece of land in the parish of Downham, near Bromley. It was tucked behind St Barnabas' Church which was consequently first to be seen by those coming up the hill. There were three ways of reaching the house: I could go along the path by the side of the church, through a gate in the high hedge and into our back garden. Or I could walk round the side of the house where a second gate led to the back door. Occasionally I went round the house to the front door, and Mummy would scold me because she was too busy to open the door to little girls who could easily go round the back and let themselves in.

So today I went through the back door into the kitchen, but there was a funny atmosphere in the house. It all seemed very quiet but somehow concentrated. Something was happening. As soon as Mum heard me, she came hurrying out of the drawing room with her best clothes on and her pearl necklace and she had lipstick too.

'Come here, Gilly,' she said. She picked up the comb from the kitchen table and started pulling the kirby grips quickly from my thick, brown and tangled hair, so it stung.

'Ow. What's happening?' I was mystified.

'There's a photographer here from the newspaper. He's come to take our photos. I need you to look tidy.' Her mouth was full of my grips as she pinned my hair and replaced the white bow.

'But why?'

'I'll tell you later.' She tugged my gymslip straight and pulled my school tie over the top.

I followed her into the drawing room and was amazed to see Mikey, my four-year-old brother, sitting on the sofa looking very good in his Sunday clothes, holding his boat. Next to him sat two-year-old Ba - well - her real name was Lizzie – but she called herself Ba because she couldn't say Elizabeth which is what Daddy always called her. She was wearing her best dress – the one that was mine when I was two, white with pink and blue smocking. Standing in the middle of the room was a man in shirt sleeves with a camera in his hand, fiddling with the metal flash device. I didn't notice much, because Ba was holding Jane.

'Why have you got Jane?' I demanded of Ba. 'You know that's not your doll! She's mine!'

'Don't be silly,' Mummy said to me. 'Ba needed a doll for the photo and yours was the nearest.'

I glared at Ba. 'Be careful with Jane!'

'Mrs Bell,' the photographer said, 'can you get out the tape measure now? I'd like to take a picture of you measuring your daughter. I imagine you will be making the children new clothes, to go to such a lonely place for so long.'

Mummy opened her sewing basket and the photographer made me stretch out my arm. She knelt down next to me and stretched out the tape measure from shoulder to wrist.

'But why do we have to do this?' I asked her quietly. 'What lonely place? Where are we going? And Grandma makes me new clothes. And Aunty Jean.'

'Be quiet, Gilly.' She used her behave-in-front-of-visitors voice. 'Just do as you're told.'

'Watch the birdie,' said the photographer.

Mikey smiled his 'I'm being good' smile, Ba stared and so did I. There wasn't a real birdie of

17

course. I knew that. The flash bulb went off. It all seemed silly to me. Everyone was pretending.

After the photographer had gone Daddy came in from the parish, wearing his clerical collar on its vestock. He was a very slim man, to Mummy's despair. She put on weight so easily and felt it was deeply unjust that he should eat so much and not weigh more than he did at eighteen. His unruly brown hair would never lie flat no matter how much he used his two black-handled hairbrushes on it. His green eyes crinkled at the corners when he was amused, which was often. I rushed up to him.

'Daddy! A photographer's been here taking our pictures!'

'Will we be in the newspaper?' asked Mikey.

'That's the general idea' he said.

'But why? What's happening?'

'I'll show you.' He fetched the big globe of the world from its stand in the study and set it on the table for us and we clustered round. Ba tried to spin it and we had to stop her.

'We're leaving St Barnabas,' he said. 'In fact, we're leaving England altogether. We're going to a place called Tristan da Cunha. It's a very tiny island in the middle of the South Atlantic Ocean, right here.' He put his finger on a cluster of dots, halfway between Capetown in South Africa and Montevideo in South America. 'They don't have a priest and they need one, so that's why we're going.'

Mikey checked where England was and surveyed the large expanse of blue between there and Tristan. 'Is that all sea?' He couldn't read yet.

'That's the North Atlantic Ocean, and Tristan is in the South Atlantic.'

'How will we get there?'

'By boat. We'll sail to Capetown in South Africa here' - he pointed '- on a very big ship. When we get there, we have to change to another smaller ship, which will take us to Tristan.'

Mikey dashed away and started jumping up and down and turning round and round. 'We're going on a ship! We're going to sail on the sea!'

'Calm down, children. Go and wash your hands. It's time for tea.'

I didn't know then that this process had been going on some time for my parents. After their deaths within a year of each other in 2009 and 2010, I found their archive boxes full of papers

going back half a century and more. I pored over them, discovering the letters Mum and Dad had regularly written to their parents, chronicling their journeys and discoveries. Only then did I find out how profoundly weary they both were at that time.

Their working day was often eighteen hours long, six days a week, during the 1950s when clergy were frequently the first port of call for those in social and emotional need. A couple of years previously she'd heard a thump in the bathroom and found Daddy collapsed on the floor. He had been feeling ill for some time but had not told her because he didn't want her to worry. She helped him into bed and called the doctor, who diagnosed exhaustion. The Bishop sent him away for a month's complete rest.

The benefits did not last long though. Our mother had had both Mikey and Lizzie over the previous five years and she was working the same hours as Daddy, endlessly answering the phone, taking messages, looking after callers, and caring for us three children. I learned she'd been very unwell too, and couldn't seem to get better. Dad had insisted on taking her to a guest house where she would not have to cook or clean. They could ill afford it on their tiny clergy stipend. Money was a constant worry, and I found that Mum's parents had been helping them, buying a new carpet for the drawing room and other things.

They were both concerned about our health too. We lived in Downham before the Clean Air Act, and so we were used to the filthy, poisonous pea-souper fogs of London which came roiling in and claimed so many lives. We were often ill, Ba and

Mikey with asthma, all of us with croup, and me with eczema treated with a smelly grey ointment from the doctor that got on all my clothes, looked dirty on my skin, and made me the subject of nasty comments at school. They both had many a broken night with us and Mum often lit a spirit stove in Mikey's bedroom, giving off vapours which helped him to breathe when he was wheezing. Ba, five years younger than me, had managed to survive diphtheria, at which point Michael and I caught measles. What panic and distress Mum must have felt especially when the doctor warned her that Ba must not catch it too, or she would die. She was frantic with worry, constantly washing her hands and clothes, and scrupulously keeping us away from our sister. Ba escaped, but a few months on she was still tiny and pale with no appetite. Mummy was always trying to coax her to eat more.

All this meant that after six demanding, exhausting years she and Dad were seriously thinking and praying about moving to another parish where our health might improve, and for some weeks had been reading the pages of clergy job vacancies at the back of the Church Times. They were willing to go anywhere but had preferences either for a parish in the north, where her parents lived and where Daddy had been a curate; or in the south-west near Dad's parents where Grandpa was also a vicar.

The day that set them off in the direction of Tristan began when Dad came in from visiting, and had a rare few minutes of quiet. Mum made him a cup of milky coffee and herself a pot of tea. Ba was in her cot for her morning sleep, Mikey was painting in the playroom next to the warm kitchen and I was at school. They both sat down at the wooden table, and Daddy read out one or two ads: then he chortled.

'I say, there's one here, Dil. Listen to this – a letter about an island called Tristan da Cunha - not sure how to say it - in the South Atlantic Ocean, where they are desperate for a Chaplain.'

Mummy set her cup down. 'Good heavens,' she said. 'I know that name.'

'What on earth do you mean?' Dad was astonished.

'My father went there in 1911,' she told him. 'It's known as the loneliest island in the world. He was a young merchant naval officer then and his ship was returning from South America. They had run short of potatoes, so they decided to call in at the island and barter for some with cotton goods. It must have made a deep impression on him because he often told us the story of his visit there. I remember it so clearly.'

'Good gracious. How extraordinary. Who would have thought that you already knew about such an obscure place?'

'I wouldn't want to take the children there, would you – so far away from our families and friends? We would be cut off from everything and everybody.'

And so Daddy moved on to look at other ads.

Over the next few weeks, they continued searching the vacancies pages together, but Dad could not get Tristan out of his head. It kept coming up when he was least expecting it. He would read about it, hear about it on the radio, somebody would mention it in a conversation. The two of them thought and prayed and discussed it and met people who had been there. They researched the climate and the education and medical facilities, and got in touch with the Revd David Neaum, the chaplain who was just about to leave the island and turned out to have three young children. This convinced them. There was no major reason why they should not go.

Finally, Dad phoned the Society for the Propagation of the Gospel, the mission society which had placed the advertisement, and was given a date for an interview on a Friday morning in London at the end of September. Afterwards, as he was still travelling home on the train, the phone rang in the parsonage and Mum answered. It was the SPG Secretary, Rev Edward Sulston. 'Please tell your husband that we are delighted to accept his application for the post of Chaplain to Tristan da Cunha. And,' he added, 'we are booking your passage for 12 January.'

Heaven knows how they got through that hectic time. Over the next three months they had to empty the parsonage, find somewhere for our furniture, pack and hand over as much as possible of the work on top of all the usual busyness. At the same time Dad would be taking St Barnabas through Christmas with all its extra services and events. Even so, a few days after his interview with SPG, he went into his study, sat down at his desk and took out three sheets of notepaper which he interleaved with two carbons. He pulled his old Remington typewriter towards him, and rolled them round the platen.

Heading the paper 'CONFIDENTIAL' he began *'My Lord Bishop: A few weeks ago I read a letter in the Church Times explaining that there was a need for a Chaplain for the people of the island of Tristan da Cunha in the South Atlantic. This recurred to my mind so often and so insistently that I concluded that it might well mean that God was calling me to do something about it.*

The upshot of this was an interview which I had at SPG House in Tufton Street last Friday morning; followed later by an invitation to accept their nomination of me as the Chaplain of Tristan for the next two or three years. The appointment is, of course, dependent upon the approval of the Archbishops' Examiners on October 20th.

My wife and I have made a careful study of the climate, conditions of life, and educational facilities for our three small children; both of us feel that God is calling us there, and we are very keen to go. We should be very happy and much encouraged if we might have our Bishop's approval and blessing on this enterprise...'

He signed the letters and sent them first-class post, one to the Bishop of Southwark and a copy to the Bishop of Woolwich.

The next day came a confidential reply from the Rt Rev Bertram Simpson, Bishop of Southwark, striking a note of caution.

'... it sounds an extremely lonely job and I cannot imagine anyone taking it on and facing the isolation unless he felt a very definite call to a very special task. If you are sure that you can face it I shall send you off with my blessing and good wishes as it is obviously a sphere which has got to be filled by

some priest who is prepared to accept its conditions; but I hope that you and your wife will give it extremely careful consideration before taking the plunge.'

As they had already given the project 'extremely careful consideration' his reservations did not weigh too much with them. They were more encouraged by the Bishop of Woolwich's letter the next day, who said *'It will be strange work and not one at which I should think one ought to stay indefinitely. But it is a great call, and may God bless you all in your going.'*

By the end of the month the announcement of Dad's appointment as SPG Chaplain to the island of Tristan da Cunha, Anglican province of South Africa, was in The Times.

From then on life was non-stop for them both. Dad made numerous visits to London in connection with all the preparations and he wrote endless letters: to the Church of England Pensions Board; to clergy charities for grants to help with all the additional expenses of taking a young family overseas; to bishops and friends and relatives; to Tristan and South African contacts; to the bank and the furniture removals. Meanwhile he continued to take services, lead courses, visit, take weddings and baptisms and funerals, and see a never-ending stream of people at the parsonage. In addition, he received sixty-three letters from well-wishers, people who wanted him to go and speak; who wanted Tristan stamps; who had some knowledge or contact with the island; and many complete strangers, including a letter from a woman offering to travel with us and look after us children on the island. My father politely refused.

Adding to the whirl of activity was the press, fascinated by this young priest taking his family to 'the loneliest island in the world'. We became minor celebrities, with interviews and photographs and news items in the local papers, and we were even on television.

I was unaware of all they had to do, and even less of the strain it must have been on them both. My main concern was for my dolls and pram. We were restricted in the amount of luggage we could take and I was told I had to leave my little family behind. I would go upstairs to my bedroom sometimes and pick up Daphne, my big china-headed doll with the painted brown hair, dressed in her flowing white robe. I treasured her because she had been given to me by parents whose little daughter had died.

'Will you be all right until I come back?' I whispered. 'I don't want to leave you, but I have to.'

Then I cuddled Patricia, the stuffed cloth black doll with her red check gingham dress and bead necklace. I didn't want her to be lonely. I hoped they would look after each other. I kissed them both, and tucked them up under their blankets in my dolls' pram. I went to my little desk with the green metal legs, got out my writing paper and wrote to Grandma in Sithney in Cornwall.

Dear Grandma and Grandpa

Mummy and Daddy say that I can't take all my dolls and my pram with me to Tristan so I am sending them to you. Will you please take care of

them for me as they are very precious? If my
cousins come to stay, they can only play with them
if they look after them.

   Lots of love from

   Gillian

At least I would be allowed to take Sambo, my black walkie-talkie doll that my nautical uncle had brought me from one of his voyages. After all, we were going to Africa, where Sambo came from.

The pace hotted up even more after Christmas as our sailing date drew nearer, because we three children went down with chickenpox. Our mother had to nurse us while she packed the wooden crates Daddy had made himself. Because we were in quarantine, we could not travel long distances, and they both struggled to work out how to see their parents before we left. With Mum's in Barrow-in-Furness in Lancashire, and Daddy's near Helston, in the end it was only possible to see them briefly when they came to London to say goodbye. Our furniture was destined for Grandpa and Grandma in Cornwall, where they had room to store it in their big vicarage.

Daddy's final church service arrived, and they were both surprised and delighted by the kindness, generosity and appreciation shown by their congregation. Downham had been a place of unremitting hard work and constant challenges, and they were both utterly exhausted and relieved to be moving on. How could they know that many years later, the young people they had helped and pastored in Downham would come and see them in Wiltshire on their golden wedding anniversary, bringing a scrap book of memories and appreciation?

'Do you remember lending your wedding dress, Dilys? – to the bride who didn't have enough money for one?'

'Do you remember your young people's group, Philip? Well – it's an old people's group now! But we still go to church and still remember the things you taught us.'

They all stayed in touch until the end of their lives.

2. STUCK IN SOUTH AFRICA

After a two-week sea voyage on the Capetown Castle, we arrived in South Africa at the end of January 1956, the height of summer. We were taken to stay in the Archbishop's palace, Bishopscourt. It was a large, light and spacious house set in gardens full of colourful flowers, with a river and ponds, and woodland at the edge of the estate. The Archbishop, Geoffrey Clayton, was looked after by white-uniformed black servants, and by a housekeeper who had her own quarters.

In the midst of this luxury the Archbishop was like a large bullfrog in a lily pond. He was a big man in his seventies, with a boxer's head and very shrewd eyes, who walked so heavily that he could be heard coming all over the house. Doors opened and closed with a crash. There were no clocks and no radio – he didn't like them and wouldn't have them. He was a bachelor with a reputation for being a woman-hater who didn't like children either.

My mother was always hypersensitive to the least breath of criticism and she was so afraid not only that she would be censured, but that we children would be considered a nuisance. We were sent to have all our meals with the housekeeper, a large white woman in her fifties, so that we did not disturb His Grace. Occasionally when he was away Mikey (now almost five) and I were allowed to go and have lunch with my parents and the Archbishop's chaplain, Roy Cowdry, in the palace dining room. It was here that Mum taught us to help ourselves carefully from the food brought round by the waiters and to practise our table manners. We always ate fruit at the end of the meal – peaches, grapes, oranges – and the highlight was washing our hands in the silver finger bowls, and drying them on the little towel the waiters had over their arms. It was a bit of an ordeal at first because I was worried about doing something wrong, but the waiters were so nice and the chaplain so relaxed that once we got used to it, we enjoyed it. My parents thought it was good for us to learn to behave in such formal surroundings.

At first Mum and Dad loved it. They were having the first real rest either of them could remember. It was warm and sunny, there was plenty of room for us all and an immense garden to play in. Mum was by training a nursery school teacher, and she soon had us doing PE on the lawn and having lessons in the three Rs. She and Mikey picked up twigs and stones and she started doing arithmetic with him, although he was only four. When I watched I could see he was very good. As for me, I read and read and read. I had taken Little Women with me and lay on my stomach on my bed in our sunny bedroom under the big windows with the sun streaming in, following their adventures, the scenes unfolding vividly in my mind's eye. One afternoon Mummy took me to see the film and there it all was – Jo lying on the hearthrug, grumbling, just as in the book. I was entranced.

However, the weeks grew into months and my parents became more and more restless. However much they enjoyed the luxury and relaxation of staying with the Archbishop, they were young, in their early thirties, and had not come all this way to do nothing. There was an additional problem in that they had run through the small amount of money they had brought with them and the mission was not paying them yet. They had been very taken aback to discover that the mission had not made any arrangements for our onward passage to Tristan. Dad spent much of his time going into Capetown to visit shipping agents to see if anybody had any sort of a ship that would drop us off at Tristan, maybe en route to Montevideo in South America. A great deal more of his time was spent writing letters, not only to his parents, family and friends but also to the mission to try and rectify the situation. Eventually they agreed not only to pay him while he was in South Africa but to backdate it to the end of January. This meant that my parents could at last start getting stores together to take with us when we finally found a passage to Tristan.

For the first time Mum and Dad came face to face with apartheid. While we were there a new edict forbade black Africans to go on the same buses as whites. The Dutch Reformed Church practised apartheid in their buildings. Black Africans were only allowed menial jobs, and lived in poverty in shacks. My parents were both horrified. Dad wrote 'Recently the S African Parliament has passed a Bill putting the non-European voters on a separate list. This increases the powers of the Government here. This is really virtually a police state with a racial policy similar to the Aryan policy formerly held by Nazi Germany. It is all very stupid as well as un-Christian ... what will be the end of this I would not like to imagine!'

They approved of the Archbishop who would have no truck with it. His cathedral had a mixed congregation, and as my father said in the same letter, he frequently broke the law by having native priests to stay with him. He could see that Dad was longing to work, so began to give him services to take in various churches around the district. My father's favourite services were with the black congregations, and my mother, with her king-sized maternal instinct, fell in love with little black babies and my father teased her by suggesting that they adopt one.

I listened and watched and formed my own opinion. The servants were Africans in white uniforms. I'd never seen servants before. They not only waited at the meal table where my parents ate with the Archbishop and his chaplain, but one of them waited at our table too in the housekeeper's quarters.

I didn't like people calling the Africans servants. It didn't seem right to me. I asked what their names were because it seemed important to know – they were normally just called 'boys'. Ours was called Francis, and Jonathan and Nicholas waited on the Archbishop and his guests. The housekeeper was always grumbling about them as if she enjoyed it, making out how bad they were, as if she were more important than they were. One day we arrived back from shopping and she came rushing out to us in the car, telling us that she was having terrible trouble with the boys and Francis had been caught stealing and she'd even had the police there. I was sent away because I wasn't supposed to be listening, but somehow, I didn't want to believe her and I felt sure there must be another side to the story. I wondered what Francis would say. I didn't trust her and didn't like her, and I didn't like having meals with her, and I didn't like the way Ba was the favourite and all she had to do was stand up in her high chair and clap her hands and shout for Francis and she would be given a chocolate Easter egg instead of the food Mikey and I had to eat. I knew my mother would not like that, so I told on Mrs Housekeeper.

When I went to the shops with my mother, I saw more of what was going on. There were always two entrances, one with a sign saying 'blankes' and the other saying 'nie-blankes'. I could work out what that meant because I knew blanke meant white. I asked her why black people and white people had to go in different doors, and she said that the white people thought that the black people were not as good as them.

I knew it. I could see them feeling superior. People were very friendly and kind to us and invited us out all the time to their houses, and some of them were the most luxurious we had ever seen, with tiled bathrooms and groomed gardens. But the white people were rich and comfortable, and they all had black servants who were poor. Daddy said they lived in shacks with metal or thatched roofs and didn't have proper electricity or running water, and he had seen them carry water in old oil or petrol cans, which they hung on wires attached to a pole on their shoulders.

They thought it was all wrong, and there were other white people who thought the same, because Daddy said he went to the House of Assembly one day and saw two white ladies standing either side of the door there, with black sashes over their shoulders and under the other arm. They were there because they were protesting at the treatment of black people. I felt proud of them. When I grew up I would do the same. Dad told me it was a policy called apartheid, and a monk called Trevor Huddleston had written a book about it called Naught for your Comfort, which had just sold out on the first day.

The Archbishop's chaplain then had to go to England because his father was very ill, so the Archbishop asked Dad to act as his chaplain while Roy Cowdry was away. He went to many different churches to take services and sometimes we went with him especially when he went to his favourite black churches. We always arrived very early so that Dad would have a lot of time to get ready, and one day I watched the children going into Sunday School. I stared at them because they looked so lovely – I knew they were very poor, but the girls were dressed in really pretty frocks with frills and hats with ribbons, and the boys all looked smart in clean shirts and ties and pressed trousers. I wondered how they managed, and I realised there was a lot I didn't know. I wanted to understand more.

One day I did, and I didn't like it. A friend took Mum and me out to Groot Constantia, the home of the first governor. It was a wonderful place with the oldest vineyards in South Africa. We'd never seen vines before and the grapes were really tiny. Then we looked round the house at all the grand furniture, and Mum especially liked the rocking cradle that was next to a big four-poster bed. I'd never seen a four-poster either. You would feel very cosy with the curtains drawn round you.

Then we went downstairs to the basement, and the lady started telling us that the governor used to have sixty slaves who worked on the land for him. Every night they were put into the basement and locked in, with no window or light so they couldn't escape. I thought of them there with their wives and the children, trapped in the hot sweaty dark.

What a terrible, terrible way to treat them. I felt my stomach start to heave and heard myself give a kind of gasp and then I started to cry and I said to Mum 'but why? Why were black people treated like that? The white people must have known it was wrong.' She put her arm round me and I looked into her face, close up to mine, her hazel eyes which just now had sadness in them. 'I think there must be a special place in heaven for black people,' she said.

When we got back to the archbishop's palace I went up to the bedroom and found Sambo lying on my bed. I picked him up and he said 'Mama' and I bent his legs so he could sit on my knee, and I put my arms round him and told him quietly 'Don't worry. I'll always look after you.'

I still have him.

3. TO TRISTAN AT LAST

I can tell from my parent's letters to their parents that they were greatly enjoying their lifestyle in Capetown. They talk so appreciatively of the friends they made, the rest they so sorely needed, the sun, the heat, the diet with all its fresh fruit, the time with us children, the services Dad took. Mikey had his fifth birthday and they gave him a crane. Ba stopped being ill, and grew chubby and tanned, to Mum's enormous relief. I had dental surgery because my adult teeth had not displaced my baby teeth. Mum also had her birthday there, and we children made her a twig tree which we had decorated with baubles made out of coloured paper from sweets.

But although they continually reassure their parents, there's underlying frustration. They had enjoyed their rest and relaxation, but were longing to get going on their own projects, Dad to his ministry on Tristan and Mum to being in her own home. Their letters are full of the endless efforts Dad made to find a passage to Tristan: he visited every shipping agency, and wrote a shirty letter to SPG for not getting our onward passage organised in advance: a letter which was then endorsed by a blunt one from His Grace the archbishop. There was even talk of our moving into a nearby parish priest's house when he went home on leave, where Dad could act as locum.

At long last, four months after arriving in Capetown, our passage to Tristan was finally confirmed. On the afternoon of 6th May 1956, we were taken by the Archbishop's driver down to the dock, where we boarded the frigate 'Transvaal'. We were met by the ship's doctor who took us below to the Sick Bay, which was to be our cabin for the next week.

SAS Transvaal

'By Jove – it's much bigger than I expected,' Dad said, pleased.

'Much bigger than our cabin in the Capetown Castle, if you can believe it,' Mum added.

'Swinging bunks!' said Mikey. 'Do we get a bunk each this time?'

'They aren't for you, I'm afraid,' she said. 'They are for Daddy and me.'

'Oh! I really want to sleep in a swinging bunk!'

'Where are we going to sleep then?' I asked, looking round.

'See this table? It's the operating table,' said the doctor. 'Look underneath.'

We found two stretcher beds which were longer than the table.

'Our heads will stick out,' I remarked.

'Or our feet,' added Mikey. But something else was bothering me.

'If this is the operating table, and people come in here to have operations, then what happens? Because we can't sleep under the table if people are being operated on!'

The doctor laughed. 'Don't worry. It's very rare for me to do any surgery. And I would do it during the day, so you would get your bed back by night-time.'

Ba kept saying 'Oooh my cot, my boo cot!' Her blue cot which had come with us from England had been dismantled at Bishopscourt, taken to the ship and the sailors had put it together again and fastened it to the floor.

Despite all this effort to make us comfortable, we did not sleep well that first night. We were still anchored in Capetown harbour, the ship's engines were running in order to generate electricity, and the blowers pushing fresh air into the room were noisy. Ba was restless and spent most of the night with Mum in her bunk.

She and Dad met the officers, who were kind and friendly, and ate in the officers' mess. This was soon to change, however. On Monday morning friends boarded to say goodbye, and after they left, the ship finally began to move. Old cine film shows us three children all in red jumpers, waving enthusiastically as the tug expertly pilots us out of the harbour. It doesn't show what happened once we reached open sea where the Indian Ocean meets the Atlantic and the waters are turbulent. The *Transvaal* had been a net-layer for submarines during the war and was built with a flat bottom, which meant that she rolled alarmingly, and after half an hour we were all feeling nauseated. Lunch was not an option and we went back to our cabin, where we took turns in being sick. Even Ba learned rapidly to be sick into her potty. Eventually the ship's doctor visited us, looking queasy himself, and confessed he was feeling as bad as everyone else. He gave us all Dramamim, after which we recovered rapidly. Mum was a poor traveller at the best of times and kept to her bunk for another couple of days while Daddy looked after us.

We loved the *Transvaal*. Even now the sound and sensation of the engines thrumming, the movement on the waves as a little ship ploughs on, and the chemical smell of diesel never fail to bring back that heady sense of excitement and adventure for me. We were allowed to go all over the ship, even up on the top deck, and for Ba the highlight every day was when Daddy took her to visit the sheep which were penned under the forward gun – stores for the small temporary contingent of scientists on Gough Island, about 250 miles from Tristan.

However, with all our toys packed away I got a bit bored. I had read all my books and went into the wardroom looking for something new to read. I discovered that there were magazines tucked into pockets on the backs of some of the chairs. I sat down on the floor behind them and began to look

40

at them. It was a new kind of book to me – there were lots of photos of ladies in them, without many clothes on. I chose the one I liked best and showed it to my mother.

I knew immediately that something very bad had happened. She looked shocked and then she said 'where did you find this?'

'In the wardroom. In those pocket-things on the backs of the chairs.'

'What pocket-things?'

I explained.

'Why do you want to read this sort of stuff?' she asked, obviously very upset. I began to feel terrible. I had obviously done something wrong but I wasn't quite sure what, so in the end I asked 'what's wrong with it?'

She started talking about how these pictures weren't good – that there were good ways and bad ways of looking at our bodies, that they had been given to us by God and we must respect them.

I felt contaminated by the books and guilty at finding them interesting, but that did not stop me. The next day, when she was on her bunk and Daddy elsewhere, I went back to the wardroom to see if I could find any more. They had all disappeared, every single one.

Dad must have had a word with the First Officer and asked him to remove the copies of 'Men Only' for the sake of the voracious reader that was his seven-year-old. A letter to his parents says cryptically 'Gillian reads everything and anything. Sometimes this can be quite helpful, and sometimes rather dangerous!'

Dad was always very sociable. He recovered quickly from sea-sickness, tucked into the meals provided in the mess and greatly enjoyed getting to know the officers. One day as they were relaxing after the evening meal with their cigarettes, he remarked on the two large and heavily-lagged pipes overhead in the mess, hanging about a foot below the ceiling.

'Ah yes,' explained the First Officer, a glint in his eyes. 'They have a purpose, you know.'

'And what's that?' asked Dad, no doubt fully aware of where the conversation might be going.

'We have an initiation ceremony. Everyone who is on their first voyage on the *Transvaal* has to be manhandled over them.'

'What are we waiting for?' said Dad, and amid much laughter they hoisted the 'dominie' bodily up to the pipes, over the top and landed him on the other side without mishap.

Dad was always good at having fun, but he was the 'dominie' or padre and his priestly ministry was his reason for being there. The Thursday of that week was Ascension Day, a major festival of the church. The Captain invited him to take a service on deck for the crew of over a hundred people, and read the Bible lesson himself. The service was held in English and translated into Afrikaans, while the crew stood silent on the deck, their feet apart to deal with the rolling of the ship, their caps off as a mark of respect. Later that day Dad asked permission to visit them in their quarters on the lower decks, and they took him to see the furnaces, engines, radio and radar. It was a multi-ethnic crew who told him how much they appreciated the

42

service being in English. Usually it was in Afrikaans, which they didn't understand.

What meant even more to them was the fact that Daddy bothered to visit them, talk to them and have a cup of tea with them. No other padre had ever done so, they said. The others always stuck with the officers in the Mess.

I know this would have meant a great deal to my father. He was never a respecter of persons and always felt passionately that faith and the church was for everyone, regardless of race or rank. His letter describes the day as 'the most wonderful and enjoyable time of the whole period at sea.'

On Friday morning after breakfast, we all helped our mother do a final packing. Mikey and I watched with fascination to see how much she could stuff into our big red and grey expanding cases. It was always a challenge to close and fasten them, and we had to clamber up on the bed and sit on the case while she wrestled with the locks. Then Ba's cot had to be taken apart, and two of the sailors took away her mattress and sewed it into canvas to keep it dry for the final journey. The weather was wet and chilly, and we were made to wear our jerseys and raincoats. Ba had a little green cape Mum had bought in Capetown, and I wore my red mac and matching sou'wester, and wished I had a mac for Sambo, and hoped he wouldn't get cold. At three o' clock in the afternoon Dad suddenly appeared in the doorway of our cabin.

'Come quick! We can see Tristan at last.'

I picked up Sambo and we all scrambled up on deck after him. Tristan was finally there.

It reared out of the racing grey water crested with foam, a great black mountain surrounded by swirling white cloud that licked down towards the sea. The cliffs soared 2,000 feet and the peak crouched on the top as if huddling from the wind and the rain.

'Why has it got that peak on the top?' I asked my father.

'Because it used to be a volcano. That's how it was made – a volcano erupted out of the sea, and when all the molten rock had cooled down, it left an island shaped like that.'

'Is it a real volcano? Will it erupt again?' I knew a bit about them. I'd seen pictures of clouds of ash, and red magma roiling downhill.

'No,' said my father. 'It's extinct.'

'What's extinct mean?' asked Mikey.

'It means it's died. It made the island and then it died – and the other islands nearby, Inaccessible and Nightingale. And Gough Island.'

We knew about Gough Island, and the temporary station there. 'Do people live on Nightingale and Inaccessible?'

'No. Only on Tristan.'

I loved those words – Inaccessible! That meant people couldn't get on to it. And Nightingale – were there nightingales on that island?

Meanwhile, the *Transvaal* was circling the island from the east side to the north. Finally, we could see it through the rain, the green plateau perched on the side of the mountain at the foot of the dark cliffs, where streams were leaping down from the heights like liquid silver filigree. We could make out the small houses, some with red metal roofs,

44

clustered together, and the rest with green roofs, more spread out.

'Stop engines,' we heard the Captain say. For the first time in six days the noise and thrumming ceased. We hung over the deck rail excitedly with Daddy filming on the cine camera, as a sailor took a hammer to the huge white anchor chain. It loosened and began to rattle swiftly through the hawse.

We ran to the stern and Daddy got out his binoculars. 'I can see longboats!' he said. 'Three of them – they are waiting near the beach just clear of the surf.'

Mum, holding Ba, eyed me. 'Gilly, you must put Sambo in Daddy's knapsack.'

'Why? I want him to see the boats.'

'You might drop him in the sea.'

Sobered, I tugged the knapsack off Daddy's back and opened the flap. I could just about shove Sambo down inside, as he said 'the boats are rowing out towards us.'

'Let me see, Daddy – please let me see!' I begged him, but when he held out the binoculars Mikey grabbed them first and put them to his eyes. I was furious.

'That's not fair,' I said to him angrily. 'I asked first.'

Mikey took no notice as usual, so I watched him closely, getting ready for my move. A moment later Mikey lifted them away from his face and I snatched them from him.

'Stop it, you two,' Mummy said. 'Michael, it's Gillian's turn.'

45

I stuck my tongue out at Mikey and started to adjust the binoculars so I could get the boats in focus, and then there they were, suddenly in close-up, looking so near and big. They were white, painted blue inside with white seats, coloured stripes all around the outside under the rowlocks. The men in them were rowing strongly, moving together like a single animal with many arms. I gave the binoculars back to Dad and watched the crew throw a rope ladder over the side of the ship. The first boat was timed exactly with the swell and arrived alongside without crashing into the ship. One of the islanders in the boat held the rope ladder which kept the boat tucked up against the ship's side, and several people swiftly climbed aboard.

Oh no, just when we thought we could start getting into the boat. I didn't want to wait, but we had to stand and be polite while these people shook hands with our parents and said hello to us and all the other things that grown-ups did which made exciting adventures annoyingly slow. But at last it was our turn and my mother was the first to go. She put a leg in its short red boot over the side of the boat and on the first rung of the ladder. I'd never been on a rope ladder and I watched carefully, on edge to have my go.

She climbed down carefully and one of the shipboard sailors shouted 'Let go, Mrs Bell - you'll be quite safe.' She sort of fell into the arms of the rowers on the boat and sat down in a wobbly way.

Then it really was our turn. To Mikey's and my great disappointment, we weren't allowed to climb down the ladder ourselves. Why did grown-ups never let us do the best things? Didn't they know how well we could climb? Instead, one of the island men appeared over the side of the ship and smiled at us, his weatherbeaten face kind and friendly, 'Who's going first?' he said.

Mikey jumped forward and at once climbed on his back. The islander went down the ladder hand over hand and the boatmen below took Mikey from him and set him down in the boat. Then at last it was my turn. I did not go down on the islander's back, but I descended the ladder carefully with the island man immediately below me on the rungs and his arms on either side of me, holding the ropes. I could not have felt safer. Finally, Ba was carried down in one arm while the islander held the rope ladder with the other, and was safely put into Mum's lap.

Mikey and I wanted to go from one side of the boat to the other, looking over at the sea – it was so near now, near enough to dangle our hands in it. But Daddy climbed down the ladder next and said we mustn't, we might make the boat tilt and then

47

it wouldn't be safe. We must sit still. Our suitcases came next and were expertly stowed. Then the men start to row us to the island.

I looked back at the grey frigate and people were waving at us from the rail. We waved back, but then I turned to face Tristan and found myself surrounded by a moving forest of arms as the islanders, dressed in coats and caps, pulled strongly on the oars while the boat was steered by a man they called John-Baptist. We watched as the island came nearer and nearer until we could see clearly the beach where we would land. There was a crowd of people there, men in dark clothes and women in cotton dresses and colourful headscarves. The cliff above the beach was lined with people too, mothers holding small children on their hips, waving as we drew nearer. Had they really all come just to say hello to us?

At the place where the white surf began to roll onto the beach, we stopped. The men held on to their oars, checking John-Baptist, checking the sea, looking behind them at the surf, sometimes rowing back with the oars while the sea spray splashed us and I could taste salt on my tongue. We were dancing on the wave.

'Why aren't we landing, Daddy?' I said.

'We's waiting,' said one of the men.

John-Baptist suddenly called 'Now' and the men all heaved at once. A strong Atlantic roller took the boat and we rode fast towards the beach until the keel was scraping the wet grey pebbles. The man in the prow of the boat threw a rope to another on the beach: he was joined by many more and together they tugged on the rope until the whole boat, with all of us and our luggage, was halfway out of the surf.

We scrambled out. We didn't even get wet feet.

Mikey and I looked at each other and we both said the same thing at the same time.

'The sand is black! Why?'

Our parents were too busy shaking hands and being kissed for us to ask them so we stored the question away for later, when Daddy told us it was black because it was volcanic. Meanwhile we watched as island men brought three ox-carts down to the beach. They were painted in reds and blues like the boats, and each cart was fastened to a pair of yoked oxen. We stayed at a safe distance from those black animals with their sharp horns.

The men, wearing long white woollen socks up to the knee with coloured stripes round the top, were heaving our tea chests up on the ox-carts until they were full, together with two big sacks.

'Oh marvellous,' said Mummy. 'That's the mail.'

'Are those sacks full of letters?' I said.

'That's right. Can you imagine having so much post to read, all at once?'

I thought about it, and I couldn't.

Eventually we set off to climb a steep path up the small cliff until we reached the plateau itself. It had stopped raining and we followed in the wake of the carts on a rough track. The green plateau grass was close-cropped, uneven and hilly, liberally scattered with grey stones, rocks and animal dung. Donkeys, cattle and sheep grazed here and there. To our right was the sea, where we could still see the *Transvaal*, a grey shape in the water. To our left, the base of the mountain soared to 2,000 feet, and now we were so close to it we could no longer see the peak. I kept looking up at the slabs of sheer black rock pointing upwards among Patches of green, deep crevices slashing the cliff at sharp angles and the streams leaping down to us.   Mike and I ran alongside the carts, watching the islanders swishing their whips in a casual way to keep the bullocks on course. We came to a big stream with a plank bridge over it.

'This is called the Big Watron,' said the schoolteacher who had come to meet us. I looked at him – he was tall and thin with a bony face and a nose that looked as if it was going to be cross with you. I said 'what does watron mean?'

'It's the island name for a stream,' he said. 'It's how they say water-run.'

Watron! My first new Tristan word. I glanced at him again – he spoke quite kindly. Maybe he wasn't too bad after all.

Then the ox-carts dipped sharply downwards into a little valley, and there was our new home.

It was a small wooden bungalow, painted battleship-grey with a metal roof, at the head of the valley or the gulch as I heard the islanders call it, which ran directly down towards the cliff top and the sea. The carts stopped outside the gate at the front, which we opened and ran into the little front garden. It was a grass plot with flower beds on both sides, surrounded by high walls and hedges of green New Zealand flax. The house looked as if it was cuddled in the middle, sheltered from any storms, cosy and ready for us.

'Daddy, why has it got two front doors?' Mikey said. We were jumping up the wooden steps on to the veranda that ran along the front.

'The screen door is a fly door,' said our father. 'It's to keep the flies out.'

'The windows have got screens too,' Mikey said to me.

'Look – the front door is in two halves,' I pointed out. 'There's a top half and a bottom half. You can shut the bottom half and open the top half and look out. Like a stable door.'

'I bet I could climb over that bottom door.'

'Mummy might not let you.'

We were about to dash off to explore more of the garden, but the doors opened and a woman came out. It was hard to tell how old she was. She was plump with dark, straight hair and dark eyes, and when I got up closer I could see that her eyelashes were quite straight. She said 'You'se very welcome' to my parents and the schoolteacher said 'this is Harriet, who's here to help you. She worked for your predecessors.'

'Hello, Harriet,' my father said. 'You come very highly recommended.'

She looked down and smiled a bit and said 'Come in,' and we went left into a sitting room with windows at the front and the back of the house, a piano, book shelves, a fire burning in the grate and a table laid for tea. We ran up to the table to see what there was.

'Cake!' Mikey said.

'The kettle is boiling, Miz Bell,' said Harriet, and we followed her into the kitchen. There was a tiny sink and wooden draining-board, and a very strange cooker. We crouched down to have a better look at the ring of blue flame burning under the kettle.

'Children, come out of the kitchen. Don't get in Harriet's way. You must be very careful with that stove.'

'But what is it?' Mikey asked.

'It's a paraffin stove. The paraffin goes into this container here,' said Dad, pointing to its shiny metal cylinder, 'then you pump it and light the gas.'

We ran into the next room, which also had windows back and front and a double bed in it with the head up against the wall. Opposite was another door, and when we went through into a small corridor, we found a bedroom on the left, on the back of the house, with two single beds.

'This is our bedroom!' I said to Mikey. 'We're sharing. Bagsy this bed' I added quickly before he could think of it, and I put Sambo on the left one. There was a small table under the window between the beds, with flowers on it in a glass jar.

'This window's got a fly screen as well,' Mikey said, bouncing up and down on his bed.

Outside our bedroom was another tiny room with a cot in it all ready for Ba, and opposite our room was the bathroom. We went in to have a look. There was a lavatory and a washbasin, and opposite the doorway a large bath. At one end of it was a copper tank which just now was roaring with a fire in it. We could see the flames licking out of the top and a chimney that went up through the roof.

'My hat,' said Daddy, looking at it. 'That's a geyser. You have to light it to get hot water. Mummy and I can have a nice hot bath before we go to bed. How kind of Harriet. She's thought of everything.'

Next to the bath was a high window, with a wooden box seat underneath. We jumped up to find out that it overlooked the veranda.

'Come on children, settle down,' said Mum as we ran around and exclaimed and looked at everything. 'It's time for tea.'

Bedtime brought new excitements. There was no electricity, so Mikey and I were given a candle in a holder each. We carried them carefully into our bedroom and set them on the table.

'Don't play with them,' warned Mum. 'It's not safe.'

We didn't, then. We lay in bed and watched the blue and yellow flames and the way the wax became like water and ran down the sides of the candle into the holder. Later when we were more used to them, we learned quite a lot about the properties of wax, as we picked some of the overflow off the sides of the candle and held them in the flame to watch them melt. Provided Mummy didn't know.

When we were finally in bed and asleep, Mum and Dad sat in their own bed with a pressure lamp alight and a sack of mail on either side of the bed, reading their letters. Daddy began an airmail to his parents and brother. 'We all leapt ashore to a shy but most glorious welcome of loving friendliness,' he wrote. 'It was almost too wonderful to believe.'

My brother Mike

'I was petrified, you know,' says Mikey now.

I look over at my brother, sitting in the bendywood chair opposite mine. We're both in our sixties. He is white-haired and white-bearded, an atheist with an interest in Buddhist practice inspired by the teaching of Thich Nhat Hanh. He has a degree in metallurgy and an MPhil in complex systems. He's been a photographer, a traveller, a local LibDem activist, an ecologist, a 2CV car repairman, a sailor, a teacher of science in secondary schools with a special interest in how people learn. He leads a life with bursts of risk and adventure, of striking out on his own, of following his passions.

'You?' I'm astonished. 'Scared? When?'

'When I had to go down the side of the ship clinging to the islander's back.'

'But why? I always assumed you would find that incredibly exciting! I was jealous of you – I wasn't allowed to do that, I had to go down the ladder on the rungs.'

'I felt terrified I might not be able to hang on. Normally, when you are on someone's back, they have their arms round your legs. However, the man had his arms on the ladder, so I was literally hanging by my arms. I thought my hands would give way and I was scared stiff.'

'I don't remember you ever being scared of anything. You always wanted to try everything, and you did. You were allowed to do things I wasn't, just because you were a boy and I was a girl even though I was older.'

'It was the first time in my life I remember thinking that sometimes I knew better than an adult. Even today I can feel the combination of terror that I might fall and anger at the adults who made me do something so obviously more dangerous on the basis that 'adults know best'.'

'And yet, you were only five. That's a lot for a little kid to take on board.'

'It's contributed to my stroppy, annoying, 'know-it-all' attitude today,' he adds, eyeing me.

'Good heavens. I've never noticed,' I tease, but sober up as I consider the implications of what he's said. 'It really could have been quite traumatic, this very little boy hanging on for dear life, scared witless that he was going to fall into the boat and smash himself against the wooden thwarts.'

Mike sniffs, the way Dad did: not because he needs to, but as a signal that he's processing ideas. I wait.

'I think it's actually been positive in the long run. It helped me do things like the green campaigning in the LibDems, the MPhil work and the evidence-based stuff on education. What they all have in common is a self-belief that I am right and these other adults haven't considered the issues properly!'

Well, that's true enough. My brother has always ploughed his own furrow, often thought he was right and at times has been surprised and annoyed when others don't see things his way.

'And to think it all started on the back of a Tristan islander, going down a rope ladder into a long boat.'

'There's another thing too,' Mike adds. 'Dad told us the volcano was extinct.'

'Well, everybody believed so at the time, but I remember thinking even then "what if they're wrong? What if the volcano comes to life?"'

'There you are, you see. It's just what I'm saying. Adults assuming they are right, when they aren't.'

'When I think about it, I realise that in some circumstances I don't trust what people say either. Especially if they tell me that I can't do something. I immediately feel rebellious and make up my mind that I'll try it anyway, and see for myself.'

'Tristan had the same effect on both of us. It just emerges differently.'

I think my brother's probably right. I also think that's why we feel closer when we discuss Tristan. He remembers it too.

4. GO BACK AND DO IT

Sometime during that first night in our new home I woke up and found my parents both in our bedroom, Dad in his striped pyjamas and Mummy in her nightdress. They had a candle which faintly lit their faces and hands, and they were standing over Mikey's bed, looking at him. I raised my head off the pillow and saw he was sound asleep, so I said 'what's the matter?'

'Ssh,' said Mum. 'It's all right. Go back to sleep.' So I did.

The next morning when I awoke Mikey was still asleep, but I could hear Mum and Dad moving around. I swung my feet out of bed and went through their empty bedroom into the kitchen and out of the front door. My bare feet made no sound on the wooden veranda as I sat on the bench which had its back against the wooden wall. I looked over the front fence, down our little valley-gulch to the sea. I could see black rocks running out into the sea in jagged lines, and could smell seaweed on the wind. Immediately outside our gate a couple of brown donkeys were grazing; one of them stopped and turned its head and looked in my direction, then began to bray.

Newly arrived, surrounded by packing cases

At that moment Daddy came out with a claw hammer in his hand.

'What are you doing here, in your pyjamas?'

'I just wanted to look. Have you seen the donkeys?'

He said 'By Jove. So that's what it was. Dilys!' he shouted, and Mummy came hurrying out, carrying Ba who was half-dressed. 'What is it?'

'You know we thought Michael had an asthma attack in the night? Well – there's our asthma attack,' he said, pointing at the donkey.

'What do you mean?' I couldn't imagine what they were talking about.

'We thought we could hear Michael wheezing in the night, like he did in Downham when he had asthma,' said Mum, sitting down next to me on the bench and putting on Ba's socks. 'But it must have been the donkey braying. It sounds so similar, especially in the middle of the night when you don't know what the noise is. Well well. So that mystery is solved, and very thankful I am too that it wasn't Mikey's asthma.'

I jumped off the bench and ran through the bungalow into our bedroom. Mikey had just woken up so I leapt on top of him and said 'Guess what – Mummy and Daddy thought you had asthma in the night – but really it was a donkey!'

'Where?' he said at once, so I told him and he went outside to have a look, and I hastily got dressed, hoping Mummy wouldn't realise that I hadn't stripped off and had a cold wash all over, which was what we were supposed to do.

The rest of that Saturday was very busy. Mikey helped Dad take the metal bands off our wooden crates and tea chests in the garden, and lever out the nails with the claw of the hammer and store the nails away carefully in an old tin they found in the small workshop at the end of the veranda. I carried in armfuls of clothes which Mum and I put away in drawers and cupboards. Harriet stripped the borrowed sheets off the beds ready for washing, and we made them up again with our own bedclothes and blankets. By supper time the rugs were on the floors, and the pink floral carpet which had been in our previous house was down in the living room.

We all went up to the little church of St Mary in the evening for a short service of thanksgiving. It was a cottage-like building, built of blocks of mountain stone which had been whitewashed, with a red corrugated metal roof which Dad later discovered leaked in several places. The islanders had not had a chaplain for nearly six months, and they turned out in force.

For this, Dad's first service, people arrived in church a good half-hour beforehand, and by the time we got there only the front row had room for Mum to sit with us ranged on either side of her. At the 8am service the following morning it was the same, with the islanders pouring into church half an hour in advance. It was a very encouraging start for Dad, and Mum enjoyed it too but for a different reason: she had left us behind, still asleep, and we woke to find Harriet and another woman sitting knitting in the kitchen. The new woman had frizzy brown hair and freckles and her name was Bertha. She was tall and always brought a sense of calm with her.

On Monday morning we started school. We had already spent much of the weekend with the English schoolmaster and his wife, whom we were told to call Uncle Ron – the man with the disapproving nose who had explained to me about watrons - and Aunty Ann and their daughter Jessica, so we had already met our teachers. Even so, I woke up scratching the eczema on my hands. I lifted the corner of the curtain nearest my bed and looked at my fingers; they were raw and sore. I went into the bathroom to run cold water over them to soothe them. I patted them dry and found my tin of pink Germolene and rubbed it in. I hoped the island children wouldn't notice the funny smell.

My parents and the schoolchildren. I am third row from the front, third from the left, with friends Minnie, Tordy and Becka. Mikey is second row from the front, near the centre, with Frankie on his right

Mikey was starting school for the first time, so after breakfast we walked up together. We climbed the concrete steps out of our sheltered garden and came out on the higher path. We turned right between flax hedges until we came to a covered wooden way on the left. It was dark inside despite the windows at regular intervals. Our feet thudded on the steps and echoed as we climbed. The corridor ran between wooden bungalows similar to ours, which had been built for people coming from what the islanders called 'the houtside world'. The bungalows were paired: the radio officer's on the left, the doctor's on the right, and so on until we reached the top. The school itself was another wooden bungalow with its own veranda, divided into three rooms. The first was for seniors, the second for juniors, and tucked away between the two at the back were the infants.

Mikey went into the infants and I to the juniors. The rooms were light and airy with windows and wooden floors, and some new desks and chairs which had just come from Capetown. I sat down in the desk assigned to me. They were all the same, although some were older than others and had words and letters carved into them. Each desk was attached to its chair, and each had a hinged lid which lifted up, with its own inkwell in the top. We started our first day of lessons, and I was glad my teacher was Aunty Ann, the schoolteacher's wife. She wasn't as frightening as Uncle Ron.

The lessons were easy but I felt shy and strange because I was stared at. A girl called Minnie had been told to look after me. She had crinkly fair hair and blue eyes, and I don't think she really knew what to do with me. At 10.30 we were told it was break, and we could go outside and play. I ran to the end of the veranda with Minnie and started down the stairs so that I could go home and see Mummy. I heard Minnie calling me so I stopped and turned round.

'Hish y'all gwine chalk dun 'ere?' she said.

I hadn't a clue what she'd just said.

'Pardon?'

She repeated it. I still didn't understand, and I felt embarrassed.

'What?'

She was leaning forward with her hand on the wooden rail that ran the length of the corridor, shadowy with the light behind her, outlining her unruly hair. I saw her shift position and then she tried again.

'Hish y'all gwine to your house?'

'Oh!' I said, relieved. 'Yes. Are you coming?'

She thudded down the steps and together we ran all the way home, where Mum gave us squash and a biscuit before sending us back.

At the end of the school day I couldn't wait to go home. It had all been so strange. The children talked in that funny accent which I couldn't understand most of the time. Mikey had only come to school for the morning as he was an infant, whereas I was a junior.

At last the bell rang. Everybody moved very fast – they lifted up their desk lids and threw in their books, but before we could go Uncle Ron, the headmaster, said

'You sly geezers, don't think you're going to get away with doing nothing! I want someone to sweep the floor.'

I stared at him. It must be that children had to sweep the classroom here. How strange.

Then I could feel fear trickling inside me because he looked at me and said 'Gillian, you can do that. Stay behind.'

Even though Minnie had been told to look after me she slid out of her seat just as fast as everyone else and they all rushed for the door, and Uncle Ron shooed them out 'Go on, you geezers! Off with you! and don't come back until tomorrow!' Then he followed them.

Why did he call them geezers? Wasn't that the thing which heated the water?

I stood up and looked round. There was nobody left. I could feel my fear not trickling any longer but filling me up like a stream. I didn't know what to do. I knew how to sweep because I'd done it for

Mummy many times but never a room as big as this and anyway, where was the broom?

I went to the back of the class to see if I could find a cupboard, but there was nothing. I looked into the infants' room but couldn't see any cubbyhole there either. I went back to my classroom and wanted to cry, because I was so scared of what might happen if I didn't do it, but I didn't know how, and I would get into trouble.

I looked outside. There was nobody anywhere, nobody to ask. I suddenly started running, along the veranda to the corridor, down all the stairs, out at the bottom, round the flax hedges and down our steps until I got into my home.

Mummy took one look at me and said 'what on earth's the matter?'

I couldn't hold it back any longer and I burst into tears, swallowing and trying to tell her. Daddy came in, and said 'what's going on?'

'Uncle Ron told me I had to stay behind and sweep the classroom, but everybody's gone and I don't know what to do and I can't find the broom and anyway, it's not fair because I'm new and it's my first day,' I sobbed. Mikey came into the room and stared at me and I stuck out my tongue at him and shouted 'it's all right for you! You're only an infant!'

Daddy took out his handkerchief and mopped my eyes. I grabbed it from him and blew my nose but I couldn't stop crying and my stomach was heaving.

He said 'you've been asked to do this job, and of course you must do it.'

I looked at him but he was blurred with tears.

'Don't make me go back, Daddy' I begged him. 'Can't you explain to Uncle Ron that because I'm new I don't know how to do it? Please Daddy, please, don't make me do it.'

'I'll come with you,' he said.

I held his big hand tightly as we approached the classroom. To my relief Uncle Ron wasn't there so he hadn't discovered yet that I hadn't done it.

'You wait here,' Dad told me. 'I'll go and find out what's going on.'

I stood in the middle of the room, dreading what Uncle Ron might say. He was rather fierce with everyone. But when he came back with Dad he only said 'let me show you where the broom's kept,' and then he told me how to put some water into a bucket from a tap, and sprinkle it over the wooden floor to lay the dust, and then start from the front of the classroom and sweep to the back. Then he and Daddy went away.

The afternoon sun was streaming through the windows and as I swept, I could see the dust motes rising and hanging in the beams. The room seemed very big, and I felt very small, and the job seemed to take a very long time, and I felt marooned and alone.

When I'd finished, I walked down the steps instead of running, and when I got home I went into our bedroom and sat on my bed and put Sambo on my lap and hugged him for a while. Then it was time for tea and Mummy said 'well, now you've done it, I don't expect you'll be asked to do it again for a while.'

I hoped she was right. That day Mum's letter to her parents says 'the children went to school and are thrilled with it.'

I hated my first day at school.

'I have gone back to this incident time and again in my life,' I tell Mike now. 'I learned, unconsciously then, more consciously since, that just because I was frightened of doing something was not a good reason for not doing it. Just because I didn't know how to do something was also not a good reason for not doing it. I began to learn conscientiousness, and courage, and reliability.'

'I remember school for a different reason.'

'Really?'

'You remember I went up from the infants to the juniors very quickly,' he goes on. 'One day I got back to school after lunch and there was just one girl there. She asked me what I had for dinner. I told her we'd had sausages and potatoes and carrots and broad beans, then I asked what she had. She replied: "I did'n get none. My Mama did'n have none." '

'That's sad. I picked up from Dad's and Mum's letters that some of the islanders were particularly poor.'

'What I remember is the feeling it gave me. It had never occurred to me that people didn't have enough food. I remember the guilt, all mixed up with a sense of being privileged, and feeling helpless, and thinking that it was unfair that I had so much and she had so little.'

'I wonder if this sort of thing helped us develop a social conscience as we grew up? I remember how angry I felt when I saw the apartheid system, because it was so unjust.'

'Could be. And the way our parents always treated everyone the same,' he remembers.

5. RATS AND DANCES

Tordy, Minnie, Becka and I were playing Grandmother's Footsteps in our garden. The one who was It stood facing the high turf wall topped by a flax hedge that divided our front garden from the vegetable patch behind it.

The others crept up behind you. If you turned round suddenly and saw somebody moving, then they became It. Short, curly-haired Tordy seemed always to be the best: the fastest and quietest.

We flopped down on the grass when Mum brought us out some squash and biscuits. She left them on a tray for us and as Minnie bit into her biscuit she said 'Hain't no school tomorrow.'

I'd missed this. 'You hain't gwin to no school?' Mikey and I had speedily mastered Tristan dialect.

'Ha's right,' said Tordy, setting down her empty glass. 'We'se gwin the Patches fuh rattin' day.'

'Rattin' day! Whassat?'

'You hain't gotta sense of a mawly,' said Tordy. 'Youssee.' I knew this phrase now. A mawly was short for mollymawk, the Tristan albatross we saw flying around. They built mud chimney-pot style nests on the ground. It wasn't polite, but it wasn't rude either.

Mikey came running through the gate with Frankie and Stanley, all of them barefoot.

Mike and Frankie Rogers

'Mikey! Minnie and Tordy dun say we'se gwin the Patches tomorrow fuh ratting' day!'

He skidded to a halt. 'I know.'

I hated it when Mikey knew something before me.

At tea time we asked Daddy and he said 'oh yes, every year there's a ratting day. You know what a pest those wretched rats are.'

We did. We could hear them running around and squealing in our attic at night. They got into people's hen runs and ate the eggs and the chicks. We always had rat and mouse traps round the house and we had to know where they were so that we did not set them off unexpectedly and get our toes or fingers caught.

'So what happens?'

'The men divide up into teams and go out to the Patches with their dogs. They find the rats' nests in the walls and then kill the rats.'

'Can we go? It's a holiday for the whole island! There's no school – and it won't be fair if everyone goes except us!'

'Of course we'll go. I'll make a picnic,' said Mum.

The plateau on Tristan is about five and a half kilometres long and less than one kilometre wide, located on the north-west side of the island which otherwise rises sheer from the sea. The settlement of houses is at the north end of the plateau, and four kilometres away at the southern end, in an area sheltered by pyramid-shaped hummocks, are the potato Patches.

Every island family had several Patches, each of which was surrounded by dry stone walls of grey rocks. Here the islanders mainly planted potatoes, but also other vegetables, although the soil was very poor. My father, much to his delight, had been given his own patch to work.

In 1882 a Yankee ship had deliberately beached itself on the island's rocky coast as part of an insurance racket, and black rats ran ashore. As is the habit of rats, they bred with alarming rapidity, swarming everywhere and eating anything they could. As a result, the islanders had instituted an annual Ratting Day, which was a public holiday.

The next day Dad set off early with the island men to walk the rough track to the Patches. Women and children followed mid-morning with picnic lunches for everyone. Mum and Harriet packed up our sandwiches, then to our excitement Harriet went off to borrow a donkey for Mum to ride. We took it in turns on the donkey, which Harriet told us was a jinny and not a jack. It was placid with a darker brown cross in the fur on its back.

'Why does it have that cross on its back?' Mikey enquired.

I knew this. 'Because of the donkey that carried Jesus into Jerusalem on the first Palm Sunday. The donkeys didn't have crosses before, but they appeared afterwards, because Jesus died on the cross.'

Mikey stroked the donkey's nose. 'How do you know?'

'People have known for ever and ever.'

But Mikey had lost interest and was watching Harriet tying on the saddle and the rope halter. 'I don't think I need a saddle to ride it, actually,' he announced.

'That's only because the island boys ride bareback and you want to be like them,' I scoffed. The boys grew up with animals and they would throw themselves on to the back of a donkey and control them by using their heels, kicking the donkey's sides, and a stick if it wouldn't move.

'Anyway,' I added, 'the saddle is for Mummy.'

As we walked and rode the stony track together out of the village, we met some of the women riding side-saddle, knitting as they went. They knitted all the time, everywhere, quite automatically and often with complicated cable patterns. The only day the needles were still was Sunday. Harriet was teaching me how to knit and I loved working socks on four needles. I never reached her level of expertise although I practised until I too could knit as I was walking along.

Harriet led the donkey with a rope halter, Mum holding Ba firmly. When it was my turn, I rode side-saddle too, and very peculiar it was, trying to get myself arranged so that I didn't keep sliding off. Mikey rode astride like the men, but when we stopped for a rest he jumped off the donkey.

'You'se gwin ride hat jinny now,' he said to Harriet. It didn't seem fair for us all to ride but not her.

'Ho no,' she said at once. 'Hi won't ride hat jinny. She's fuh Miz Bell.'

'But you can have a turn too,' said Mum, who was giving Ba a drink. But Harriet refused and we couldn't persuade her.

The walk lasted about an hour and a half. After a while we dropped into the stony darkness of Hottentot Gulch, the donkey picking its way daintily down the steep sides slippery with scree, along the bottom and up the other side to the light and the green grass of the plateau once again, with the mountain always on our left and the sea on our right.

'Why is it called Hottentot Gulch?' I asked idly.

'I'm not sure,' said Mummy vaguely, carrying Ba for a while as her little legs couldn't walk far. We usually went to Dad if we wanted facts. But then she added 'I think the Hottentots were a South African tribe. You'll have to look it up in the encyclopaedia when we get home.'

She was always telling us to look things up in the encyclopaedia. She and Daddy had made sure to bring a set to Tristan for us to use.

'But did the Hottentot people come here?'

'I don't know. Look it up.'

We walked and rode on. Today was windy and the sky was full of racing clouds, while the sea in shades of grey and blue tossed white manes and the dangerous swell ran fast and deep. It had been too windy for the men to go fishing, which was good. It meant everyone could go to the ratting without missing a day's catch, which was needed to fill their quota for export to South Africa.

Halfway through the walk we skirted a steep green pyramidal mound called Hillpiece, criss-crossed with the sheep tracks that threaded the island. The seaward-side dropped straight into the ocean, where a couple of hunks of cliff had become separated from the island and stood free, known as The Hardies. The sheep tracks on Hillpiece made Mikey and me long to climb it, but we were very rarely allowed to do so; Dad always had a lot of gardening work in hand which we were expected to share.

By the time we arrived at the Patches the ratting was well under way. The island boys, our schoolmates, were absorbed in the hunt with their fathers and uncles. We saw Dad and waved and shouted: he came over to fetch Mikey and me so we could go and watch.

We picked our way over the uneven turf to one of the walls where the ratting was happening, although the teams were at work all over the Patches. The men and their dogs were methodically pulling down sections of the walls with their bare hands and then the dogs went in after the rats with shouts of encouragement from their owners. Our cine film shows one of the men holding several rats by their tails, one still alive and squealing.

Most of the time the dogs killed them instantly. As they went, the men collected the rats in bags. There was a reason for that.

We weren't scared or alienated. It was normal life, what people did, and we were fascinated. Watching was hugely exciting. Mikey and I climbed on a little mound to get a better view: as the wall was broken down and the rats ran out and the dogs chased them, Mikey was hopping up and down next to me.

'Look – there's one there – I don't think the dogs have seen it!'

'Yes they have – that one's chasing it.'

'I don't think it's going to catch it … '

'Yes he is – they are really clever. They know just what the rat will do.'

'I can't see what's happening!' Mikey complained, and a minute later he disappeared. Tearing my attention from the hunt I glanced round and he'd slipped down the hummock into a muddy pool at the bottom.

'Daddy!' I yelled, and scrambled down after him. It was only a shallow pool so there was no real danger, but Mikey was soaked and covered in mud and grit. Filthy from head to foot, we took him back to my mother who said

'Oh Mikey! Now what have you done? What a sight you are! What are we going to do? I've got no clean clothes for you at all.'

Harriet was sitting on the grass next to my mother and Ba, placidly knitting socks on four

74

needles. 'Hi go and hask somebody – maybe they's got dry close,' she said, and came back a few minutes later with a set of boy's clothes from one of the women. Mum started to strip Mikey but he looked round and saw a group of boys watching. Mummy hadn't noticed them and didn't understand why he was so insistent that she kept him covered as she changed him. He never normally made a fuss. We weren't allowed to at home.

'Don't be a silly boy,' she said briskly. 'It doesn't matter. Everyone knows what little boys look like. Nobody here will mind.'

He clutched Mum's green jacket firmly in front of him and refused to budge, and she had to stand up behind him and dress him from the back. Once the shorts were pulled up he was fine, but when I looked round I saw the boys pointing and laughing and making comments to each other.

I knew that Mikey would get teased and I thought about my mother's attitude, and the boys' attitude, and the gap between them, and how Mummy must understand it from Mikey's point of view.

'Those boys are laughing,' I said.

'Then they are just silly,' she said vigorously, although she glanced over at the boys, and I somehow knew she quickly understood how Mikey was feeling. She made no further comment about it, combing her fingers through the thick dirt in his fair hair. 'There you are. You'll do until I can get you home, then you can have a bath and I'll give you a good scrub.'

We sat down in the sun and the wind and ate our sandwiches, looking out over the changing colours in the ocean in front of us, the mountain at our back. It was a clear day and my father pointed to a dark shape on the horizon. 'Look! You can see Inaccessible Island today.'

'Is it really inaccessible?' I asked, in-between large bites of Marmite sandwich in one hand and a hard-boiled egg dipped in salt in the other. It was my favourite combination. 'Does it mean that nobody can get there?'

'Pretty much,' he replied. 'People can go, but it's difficult and dangerous to get ashore and there's no safe place to leave the boats. It's a different matter on Nightingale island.'

'Where's that?' asked Mikey. 'Can we see it from Tristan?'

'No – it's behind the mountain. But the islanders go there every so often, to collect penguin eggs and guano.'

'What's guano?'

'It's penguin manure,' he explained. 'The soil here is so poor that the islanders need something to enrich it so that the potatoes will grow better. Guano, and of course the cattle manure.'

We already knew about cattle manure. Dad needed it for our garden at home. He would send us out with our buckets and shovels, to collect the cow pats lying everywhere round the houses in the settlement. It was not a job I enjoyed. Instead of being able to collect the nice dry pats that came up easily, my father insisted on the wettest and freshest. He said it was much better for the garden. I used to argue and complain, but it never got me anywhere. With his usual dictum of 'if he will not work let him not eat,' culled from St Paul, I was scolded and sent off anyway. It was best if I did it with my friend Minnie. She didn't complain and she was good at it.

Eventually the ratting excitement was at an end and we were taken home to be bathed and fed. But the fun wasn't over, because first we had the children's dance, and then the adults had theirs.

As I was drying myself with a towel after my bath, Mummy told me I had to open the children's dance. I was still wet but I stopped dead, horrified, the towel hanging from my hand. We'd been to several dances and it was easy enough – by and large the islanders got into couples, then shuffled round the floor, the women going backwards guided by the men - rather in the way they rowed a boat. We children simply copied them. But I hated the thought of being stared at, of being out there in the middle of the floor with everyone watching.

'Do I have to?' I said plaintively.

'Yes you do. There's no choice.'

'But I don't want to! All the children will laugh at me!'

'Nonsense. Why should they? You'll do it very nicely. And you can wear your bridesmaid's dress,' she added persuasively.

Now this cheered me up. Not long before we'd left England for Tristan, I had been bridesmaid to one of my mother's brothers, and had been made a floor-length white nylon dress with little gold velvet dots all over it. It was a simple dress with cap sleeves edged in lace and a narrow gold velvet sash around the waist. My mother had cut it down, putting a huge hem on it so that I could go on wearing it as I grew. I put it on over a white petticoat, followed by white socks and the white sandals which only just fitted me. Then my mother said 'sit still' and I sat on a kitchen chair, while she took her long-tailed comb and started work on my thick brown hair, still damp from the bath. Where the front sections had already dried, she spat on her fingers and then pulled the hair around them, curling as she went. My hair was parted on the girl's side – Mikey had his on the boy's – and the final touch was a kirby grip pushed firmly in at the side of my head and a white ribbon attached to it.

'There,' said my mother. 'You look very nice. Mikey, come here. And don't you dare go outside. I don't have time to wash you again if you get dirty before the dance.'

'Don't want to go to the stupid dance anyway,' he grumbled. 'I hate dances.'

'The other boys will be there.'

'Can I go and stand with them?'

'If you're good, sit still and keep clean.'

'Anyway,' I added, 'you've got to do the first dance with me.'

Mikey looked at me, his blue eyes mutinous. 'Shan't.'

'Well, you've got to. If I've got to, you've got to.'

'I won't. I'm not going to dance at all.'

'Mummy!' I said anxiously. 'Tell him he's got to!'

But her arguments and pleas fell on deaf ears. Mikey got down from the chair, went into the bedroom and shut the door. I was almost in tears.

'It's not fair!' I stormed at my mother. 'Why have I got to do it but not Mikey?'

'He's younger than you and he's going through a shy phase,' she said in her soothing voice, which meant that I would have to do as I was told and that was that. I went up to the dance with fear leaping in my stomach, all pleasure spoilt.

Before the village hall was built, communal activities took place in the schoolroom where we juniors normally had our classes. The desks had all been moved out apart from chairs set around the edges, and when we got there somebody was already playing records on the record player. The girls were sitting along one wall, in their best dresses like me. I spotted Minnie and Tordy and went over to them and they said 'Hish y'all gonna hopen the dance?' and nudged me.

'Hi don' wanna,' I said crossly.

'You'se got to,' they giggled.

Over the other side of the room the boys were wearing their Sunday clothes, some with long white socks and home-made moccasins, making comments to each other and looking at us. Aunty Ann, the headmaster's wife, wearing a blue smock to cover her pregnancy, was setting up a table with other mothers, putting out orange squash and biscuits for when we got thirsty.

At length Uncle Ron, the headmaster, walked into the middle of the room and eyed us. 'Now then, you geezers!' he said. 'So you're ready for your dance, are you? You lucky children, you!'

He looked over at me and my heart sank. So there really was no escape. I knew I had to choose one of the boys to be my partner in order to open

79

the children's dance and I was afraid of what the children would say to me and how much teasing I would have to endure. I spotted Martin among the boys, the administrator's son, a friend from the expatriate 'station' who was a year older than me. He was a chunky boy with dark hair cut short, and tonight he was wearing grey shorts, matching jacket, a shirt and tie and I had to admit he looked very smart.

The first bit was the worst. Tordy and Minnie shoved me in the back and I had to walk all across the empty space in the middle of the room. Martin saw me coming and I could see he realised I was going to ask him. As I feared, some of the boys dug each other in the ribs and sniggered, but it was too late by then.

When I reached Martin, I realised he was not nearly as nervous as me. His confidence gave me some of my own, and we walked a little way into the room. Uncle Ron put the needle down on the record and we began our shuffle.

I was so relieved to see how quickly the other children also formed into couples and followed us.

I wasn't as conspicuous and that was infinitely better. I felt less self-conscious and began to enjoy it, and had dances with other boys as well.

When all the dancing was over and the children were leaving, I begged my parents to let me stay for the beginning of the grown-ups' dance. I knew they had been asked to open it and I badly wanted to watch. Mum agreed, 'provided you go straight home to bed when I tell you.'

I promised. Mikey and Ba went home with Harriet, but I stayed and watched as the adults arrived: the South Africans from the 'station' where we lived with the other expatriates; the island women in colourful skirts and blouses they had made themselves; both men and women wearing the knee-length white island-knitted stockings that by now were so familiar because we wore them ourselves.

The men stood in a line in the middle of the room, chatting idly, but I could see their eyes darting over the women. They were choosing. Who? What made them choose one girl and not another?

It was obvious that they were all looking forward to this dance after their long day at the Patches. We waited until the administrator, Martin's father, came into the hall and the hubbub died down. He announced the prizes for the ratting day winners: one for the team who had caught the most rats, and another for the team which the rat with the longest tail. Everyone clapped and commented to each other.

I squatted on the floor with the women, next to Granny Mary who was wearing a new headscarf over her grey bun for the occasion. She had knitted me some socks which I loved. She patted me on the shoulder. 'You sit there, my lil girl,' she said. 'You'se hall right with Granny Mary.' She was large and comfortable and kind and a great friend of Mum.

I couldn't wait to see my parents dance. I had been intrigued to discover that although Mum loved dancing and was very good at it, my father hated it, had no sense of rhythm and couldn't dance for toffee. He was completely unmusical, being tone-deaf, and was the despair of church organists all his life. I wondered what would happen. Would people laugh at Daddy? I hoped not.

Gradually the room hushed, the gramophone was wound up and the record started to play. My mother, looking pretty in her best pink dress with the dropped waist and pleated skirt, sat on an upright chair in the middle of the floor. My father in his grey suit approached her and held out a hand, inviting her to dance with him.

My mother acted very shy. She looked down and shook her head. A titter went round the room. Nobody was expecting this.

My father feigned puzzlement. Then he put his hand in his jacket pocket and took out a small chocolate bar. He approached her and held it out. She looked at it, hesitated, then shook her head again.

By this time everyone was laughing. Dad turned round to the men with a gesture of despair, gesticulating to them for advice. They shook their heads too.

He approached my mother again, who had coyly turned half-away from him on her chair. He walked round in front of her and this time produced two chocolate bars. My mother looked at them, pretended to think, then shook her head again.

Daddy pantomimed frustration, then put up a finger as if he had just thought of a solution. He tucked his hand inside his jacket, and produced a very large chocolate bar tied with a red ribbon. Again he offered it to Mum, and this time she nodded her head. Everyone cheered.

'That faather do be so funny,' I heard one of the women say. He and my mother busily shuffled round the floor to the few remaining bars of music, a triumph of necessity over inability.

Then I was sent home to bed.

'Dad's sense of humour was off the charts,' I say to Mike now. The thought of it puts a smile on my face. 'All that fooling around!'

'It was very much part of our childhood. Do you remember he would sit at the table sometimes and just talk a whole lot of gobbldeygook – made-up words?'

'Ba got really good at talking that language back to him.'

'And then he used to say outrageous things with an absolutely straight face, and people couldn't tell if he was joking or not -' adds Mike.

'- until Mum called him an arch-wangler or something!'

'Yes – and it was all the funnier because it was 'Faather Bell' acting the fool. Something to do with their priest being human! The islanders enjoyed his sense of humour.'

'They did,' I reflect, 'but there was more to it than that. Because Dad was tone-deaf and had no sense of rhythm and couldn't dance, he had to find a way round that, and he used humour. It was how he handled this particular disability of is. As I suppose we would call it now.'

I go back to something else that has struck me.

'I still wonder why you were let off dancing and I wasn't. It's all very well for Mum to say that you were going through a shy phase, but that doesn't seem to have influenced her when it came to my shyness.'

'I think it was much more to do with the fact that I was more stubborn than you.'

'How do you mean?'

'Mum knew that if I had made up my mind not to do something, I absolutely refused point-blank to do it. Even if she had

got me up to the dance and told me to do it, she was well aware that I would simply refuse.'

'Wonder why that didn't work for me?'

'You were more malleable. Mum knew if she pushed you, you would do it.'

I digest this new piece of information about my younger self. I think it's probably true, although for some reason I want to resist it.

'I don't like to think of myself as being pushed around. It's more to do with knowing that Mum was desperate to please everyone, and that I was a part of that. If I refused then it would have reflected on her and Dad, and that worried me. And then the stuff I'd learnt on my first day at school, of having to do something whether I liked it or not.'

'Quite possibly. I was never that aware of how other people felt.'

'Yes, you generally lived in your own little world.'

'Still do ...'

That's true enough.

6. FIRST MAIL

I kept waking up and going back to sleep because I could hear Daddy switching the radio on and off. It crackled and then I heard Mr Meyer, the radio officer, talking to the fishing ship Frances Repetto as she sailed from Capetown towards Tristan with our very first mail. We'd had none since May when we first arrived, months ago now. It was a long time not to have any news of our families. I looked at my watch which I always left on the chest of drawers under the window between Mikey's bed and mine – 6am.

I dozed off, but the radio crackled again in the next bedroom and this time my watch said 7 o'clock. I could hear my mother being sick in the bathroom. We were not allowed to tell anyone yet, but she was pregnant and next June we were to have a new baby brother or sister. I knew I'd love to have our own baby. I spent as much time as I can with Aunty Anne's baby Lucas– he was so lovely, chubby and happy – I was even knitting him a pair of mittens, with Harriet showing me how to do the tricky bits.

Poor Mummy. She had been sick every day for weeks and I had got worried, which was why she had to tell us. She had stopped now, and water was running, so I guessed she was having a wash. Her mouth must feel horrible after all that sick. Mine always did when I was seasick.

I heard the front screen door slam shut on its spring, and Daddy's footsteps across the pebbles in front of our veranda. Why was he going to church so early? Then I heard the creak of the screen door again. That must be Harriet arriving.

I climbed out of bed and went through to my mother's bedroom, where she was back in bed. She'd opened the curtains and the window a little way so a fresh breeze was blowing in, and had pulled the sheet straight with the pink embroidered coverlet over the top, and put on a clean nightdress and combed her hair, but she still looked pale and her eyes were blurry.

'Are you all right, Mummy?'

'Yes darling, I'm fine. I'm always sick when I'm expecting a baby, you know. The first three months are the worst.'

'Harriet's here – shall I ask her to bring you a cup of tea?'

'That would be lovely.'

I had to go through their bedroom to get to the kitchen and dining room, and sure enough Harriet was there, today in a green canteen cardigan buttoned up the front and a long cotton skirt over white island socks she'd knitted herself. She was pumping up the paraffin gas stove and putting on a kettle to boil.

'Mummy says please can she have a cup of tea?'

Harriet said 'Yes, and I'll make youse tea too. Y'all get dressed and come for youse breakfast.'

I went back to see my mother and asked 'Why did Daddy go out so early? The first service isn't till 8 o' clock.'

'Ah yes, usually. But with the ship coming, and the island men wanting to row out to her and get the mail and the stores, Daddy wanted to give them an early service before they went.'

I went to her window and looked out to the racing sea, its waves whipped into white tops in the lively wind. Grey cloud hovered and flew over the sea and swirled around our house. The mist had come down the mountain and covered our plateau and was full of rain, and I had to strain my eyes to see anything through the mesh of the fly screen.

'I can't see anything. Where is the Frances Repetto?'

'That's the problem – it's so stormy and the visibility is so bad that she didn't even know where she was, last time Daddy had the radio on. Maybe Mr Meyer will be at early church and have some more news.'

I went back to the bedroom and found Mikey still asleep – I shook him and said 'Wake up! The Frances Repetto doesn't even know where she is, the visibility is so bad!'

Mikey was immediately awake.

'How do you know?'

'Radio message,' I told him succinctly, rather pleased to be first with the news. 'Bagsy first wash' and I rushed into the bathroom before he could think of it, while he scampered into Mummy's room to look through the window. As I ran the cold tap the rain lashed down, drumming noisily on our metal roof, and the high green flax hedges round the house shushed and bowed and crackled in the wind.

We were not allowed a warm wash in the morning. We always had to use cold water – Mummy and Daddy said it would toughen us up, and look, we've not had any colds since we came here. I squeezed out my flannel and rubbed it over my face and body, my bare skin shrinking from the chill. I got over it as fast as possible and then grabbed my towel and dried myself vigorously to warm up. I ran back to the bedroom, past Ba who was standing in her cot in her room, and started pulling on my clothes rapidly. I couldn't wear trousers today – none of the girls or women ever wore trousers to church – but I did put on my vest under my dress and dug out a ganzey, a cardigan knitted by Harriet for me.

Mikey came into the bedroom as I went out – he had been out on the veranda in his pyjamas in the wind and rain and his fair curly hair was even messier than when he woke up. 'I reckon we'll be able to see it soon. The cloud is lifting over the sea.'

I lifted Ba out of her cot, stripped her of her night things and took her into the bathroom to give her a quick wash. She got cold water too. Then back to her bedroom where I dug out clean clothes from a drawer and rapidly dressed her. I did it quite often, especially once Mum started to be sick.

'Time for breakfast,' I told her.

Daddy came back from early service and sat down with us in the kitchen for breakfast, where we ate Harriet's sticky porridge and had home-made bread with butter and Marmite. We couldn't see the sea from our table, so as soon as we'd finished, we jumped up and ran outside again to check the weather.

'Children,' said Dad. 'Come back here and clear the table for Harriet. I know it's very exciting but that's no excuse to leave her with all the work,' and he took another cup of tea into the bedroom for Mum, who then got up and dressed, ate some cold dry toast, pronounced herself feeling better, and joined us on the veranda where the ship was still not visible.

Daddy got the really big, powerful binoculars that were in the house when we arrived and lifted them to his eyes. We took it in turns to look, but still we could see nothing. We cleaned our teeth and got ready for children's church at 11am: Daddy had gone ahead, taking the binoculars with him.

Just as we were about to set off a huge storm erupted all around us, driving the rain into the veranda and us indoors, shrieking, out of its way. The noise of the rain on the corrugated iron roof was so loud we had to shout to hear each other. We were laughing and telling silly jokes – we loved this sort of weather, it was so wild. Mum made us put on our macs and sou-westers, but when we left the house the rain stopped as suddenly as it started and the wind died. As we walked up to church we kept turning round to look at the sea, and by the time we reached St Mary's Mikey said 'I can see it.'

'No you can't,' I said at once, annoyed that he saw it first. 'Where is it then?'

'There,' he said, pointing towards the horizon. 'It's just a little dot.'

I stared hard, and he was right: a small grey shape, so far away we could barely see it moving.

But it was too exciting to be annoyed for long. We went into church with all the other children, and although I kept looking out of the window surreptitiously on the seaward side, nobody else seemed to and so, rather ashamed of my wandering mind, I settled down and paid attention like everyone else. We were all looking smart. Everyone got dressed up for church. We girls were in our best dresses, and I saw Becka had a new beret, while Emmie was wearing her usual kappy and chewing her finger. The boys in jackets or ganzies and shirts with long trousers, their hair slicked down with water.

Afterwards when everyone had gone Mikey and I went into the vestry as usual to help Dad put everything away. I looked at Daddy's metal comb on the tiny windowledge in the vestry, and exclaimed to Mikey 'look at these silver fish!' He slid his finger under one of them and watched it running over his hand, and said 'I wonder why they're called silver fish – they don't look like fish at all' while I picked up the water in the little basin that Dad had used to wash his hands at Communion, and went outside to throw it on the ground.

'Why do we have to throw it on the ground?'

'It's been used for a special purpose, so we give it back to God's creation.'

'I see,' I said, impressed.

'Come on,' said Mikey impatiently and we left Daddy to lock the vestry door while he tore off down the track home, leaving me to follow as quickly as I could with Ba. I could see the ship steaming closer and closer to the shore. She was only small compared with some of the ships which visited, which were too scared to come close to the island in case they ran aground. The Frances Repetto knew Tristan waters very well, because she was our regular fishing vessel, sailing between Capetown and us during the spring and summer to take the canned rock lobster off the island to sell in South Africa, bringing our mail, and other stores for the island shop that everyone called the canteen.

When we got home I found Mikey outside up the side of our valley. 'She's dropping anchor,' he observed, and she was now close enough for us to see the hawser running out through the cat hole in the prow, and faintly hear it rattle. The ship stopped and swung into the wind, just opposite Big Beach from where they would launch the boats. The wind had dropped and the rain was merely mizzle.

We rushed indoors and shouted 'Mummy! The ship's dropped anchor and she's really close in!'

'Wash your hands,' said our mother firmly, tying a bib round Ba for her lunch. 'Nothing's going to happen for a little while. We'll get our mail as soon as possible, but first we're going to have a special lunch to celebrate.'

The table was all set with our best table mats. 'Mmm!' I said, spotting what was in our glasses. 'Fresh grapefruit juice!'

'It's a little treat,' she said. 'It's the last of the grapefruit we brought with us from Capetown, so make the most of it.'

We gobbled our pork chops and vegetables despite her telling us not to, rapidly helped Harriet to wash and dry the dishes, then at last we were free to go outside with Dad and the binoculars, and climb the side of our gulch from where we could see Big Beach. It took a little practice, to settle the eye pieces on our eyes and get the focus right, and then to keep the long curve of Big Beach in the centre of the lens, where the waves were breaking on the black sand.

'Look – the boat's setting out from Big Beach! '

'The men are rowing really hard – those are strong waves,' I said, snatching the glasses from Mikey.

'Don't snatch,' said Daddy automatically. 'Give them back to me now.'

At 2pm we put on our rainwear again and Mikey and I ran and skipped over the rough plateau terrain with our father to the beach. There was already a crowd of islanders on the upper beach, the women standing knitting, looking out to where the ship rocked and swung at anchor with the longboat fastened to our side of her, in the lee of the ship. Because she was so close in, we could see the sacks of mail being handed down over the side of the ship into the boat, along with other stores.

We said hello to the islanders but ran past them down onto the beach itself with its small canning factory.

'They're starting to row back!' announced Mikey and at the same time the boys and men all came out of the factory. They made their way unhurriedly down the beach as the boat approached the surf rolling on to the shore.

We could see the cox watching warily. We knew from our own arrival on the island that he had to choose exactly the right moment to bring in the boat so that it did not capsize.

'They're coming now' said Mikey and started jumping up and down, but the cox decided against it and the islanders rowed back on their oars, hovering on the edge of the swell as they had done when bringing us to the island from the ship. They tried again, but the surf leapt up over the boat and soaked everyone, and the men rowed back hard once more. Every eye was on them and we were learning rapidly how they judged the moment precisely when the boat was in the right position and the wave was at the right point and height. The third time they heaved on their oars and surfed on to the beach. Some of the factory men ran forward with a wire rope attached to the only powered cable on the island, and the longboat was winched high up the beach to be upturned later and lashed down at a safe distance from the sea in a more sheltered nook where the gales would not damage it.

One of the men had yoked his bullocks to his cart which stood ready on the beach. The precious sacks of mail were heaved into the cart along with some other oddly-shaped bundles.

'What are those, Daddy?'

'They're fodder for the prize bull.'

'Well why does he need it? Why can't he eat grass like the cows?'

'Because the grass is very poor here, and there isn't enough to feed all the animals. The cows get thin and sick, then they don't have healthy calves. We need their milk and meat to survive here. The

94

problem is that all the animals feed all over the plateau.'

'Well how will feeding the bull help then, if there isn't enough grass and the cows get sick and thin?'

'That's a good question.'

That was the year when the island council decided to fence off some of the pasturage, to allow the grass a chance to grow. As well as cattle, there were sheep, donkeys, pigs, geese and poultry to feed.

We followed the bullocks up the track from the beach to the plateau, their hooves slipping on the sand and gripping on the rocks. They strained forward to pull the cart, their owner at their heads, flicking his whip. At the top they increased speed and took the track back to the settlement.

'Where are they taking the mail?' I asked.

'To the library to be sorted.'

'A library! I didn't know there was a library here – why did nobody tell me?' I exclaimed, agog at the thought of so many books to read.

'Well, they are mostly for grownups.'

'Oh.' That probably meant they would police my reading. I didn't actually make a decision, but somewhere I registered that one day I would go there on my own and look at the books. But not today. At this moment the arrival of the mail was too exhilarating, and now we had arrived at the library. The islanders unloaded the cart and took the sacks into the low wooden building.

'Please Daddy can I come and watch?'

'No, you need to go home and help Mummy.'

'Please, please,' I begged, 'you know I'm good at reading and I can help with the sorting.'

He looked at me and hesitated. Mikey had already run back home.

'All right then. Just for a little while.'

We went into the library with its wooden floor and walls and a metal roof like the other expat houses. I looked round eagerly at the tall bookcases which carried dusty books. They had the neglected look of those which are seldom read and there was a musty smell.

The islanders were already sitting on chairs at one end of the room, and the rest of the space was occupied by two tables. On the far wall empty sacks were hanging from pegs, with the name of an expatriate or 'station' family over the top of each. One of the men carried in the first sack, undid the neck and emptied it out onto the table. The letters and parcels slithered everywhere, large and small and square and cylindrical, white and brown envelopes, blue airletters. We found places round the edge of the table where some of the expats were already sorting. Letters for the islanders went on the next table and one of the station wives called out the names:

'Sidney Glass. Cheseldon Rogers. Mrs Martha Repetto.'

Every time a name was called, she handed a letter over to the waiting islanders. More exciting than this was recognising our own name on so many of them. I took a handful and began to sort, putting the station letters into the sacks on the wall.

The sorting took nearly two hours, and finally it was time to take our own sack home, bulging haphazardly with months of mail. Daddy heaved it onto his back and I trotted along by his side. Mikey heard our feet on the pebbles and shot out of the house, followed by Ba who didn't understand what was going on but knew it was important. He held open the screen door for us so that it would not bang shut on its spring, and we followed Daddy in, to find our mother waiting in the sitting room.

'Here we are at last, the long-awaited mail!' he said, and emptied the sack all over the floor. Mikey and I pounced on small cylindrical packets wrapped in brown paper.

'What are these?'

'They're comics for you – somebody has kindly offered to send them to you regularly.'

'My hat!' said Daddy. 'That should keep you quiet for a while!'

'Can we open them now?'

'Let's get it all sorted first,' said our mother. 'Put all the comics under the settee. Then you can read a few in bed after supper.'

Ready for bed

'Thrilling!' I exclaimed and Mikey and I started clawing out the distinctive comic bundles from the rest of the post, giving some to Ba and showing her how to stack them under the settee. Eagle and Girl, Swift and Robin.

'You can probably read some of the Robins by now,' I told Mikey, thinking how lucky I was to have all of the rest of them to myself. He was five, and very good at sums but not so good at reading yet. 'I'll read some to you if you like when we're in bed.'

'I want a tory too,' said Ba who was now three. She'd already had her bath and was in her long white and blue spotted nightgown, her golden-brown curls brushed and shiny.

'OK – I'll read you a tory too,' I said. I did a lot of that because she loved it and I enjoyed it.

'Don't say OK,' said my mother, but her attention was on the letters in her hands.

'Why not?'

'It's slang.'

'What's wrong with slang?'

'It's not good English. Now hurry up with your sorting and then we can have tea. The quicker it's done the sooner you can start reading,' she said, looking up from her letters and eyeing me knowledgably. She knew I could hardly bear to wait.

Finally, it was all sorted – eighty letters and forty packets mainly for our parents, from our grandparents, relatives and friends in England, and a large number from keen philatelists all over the world, wanting first-day covers and Tristan stamps.

After tea we had our baths as usual, said our prayers with our parents and then scrambled into bed.

There was nothing to rival that moment, that magical moment, when I could start tearing off the perforated strip at one end of the comic cover, impatiently pulling it away, then unrolling the comic and smoothing it out. I put aside the Swifts and Girls for myself later, but first I did what I had promised. Ba climbed into bed with me and Mikey jumped on too, and I read a Robin from beginning to end, pointing to the pictures as we went so that they could follow.

Eventually Mum took Ba to her cot in the next room, but let us have the candles alight for what she called a few more minutes. I was banking on her being so interested in her own letters she would forget about us for a while. Mikey and I lay on our stomachs on my bed and went through a Swift before she caught up with us, and made us blow out the candles, and took our torches away. She knew what I would do if she didn't. Reluctantly we settled down to sleep, the comics and papers on the floor by our bedsides ready for the morning.

My parents sat up much later, trawling through their post, putting them in chronological order, slitting open the air letters, occasionally reading sections out to each other, exclaiming that Ruth had had her baby, and why had Derek still not written?

This epistolary interlude continued until after midnight, wrote my father, when we decided to leave the magazines until the next day and go to bed!

❀❀❀

'One of the things that bothers me,' I say to Mike, 'is the way we, the' houtside worl'' or station people, the expatriates, did all the sorting of the mail while the islanders sat there, waiting to be called. I rebel over that idea. It seems so colonial – as if the islanders couldn't do it themselves, when of course they could.'

Mike does that sniff, and ponders. 'I'm not sure that's it. I think it's much more likely that the vast majority of the mail was for the expats, so it made sense for them to do the sorting.'

'Hmm. Not sure. I guess we'll never know. Do you remember getting all the comics?'

'Yes. They were a real feature of life, weren't they – we read them over and over until we knew some of them by heart.'

'You were good at maths but slow at learning to read – did the comics help with that?'

'They must have. I've discovered since then that I have some characteristics of mild dyslexia, so the short line lengths of prose and the images were exactly what I needed.'

'Do you remember Dan Dare in the Eagle? And when the space force lands on Mars? And it appears to be uninhabited? And they shout to see if there's anyone around?'

Mike cocks an eyebrow at me and we both know what's coming next. A vivid image of cartoon creatures suddenly appearing out of holes in the ground occupies my mind with speech bubbles over their heads.

"'You needn't shout ..'"

"'We're not deaf ...'"

"'Martians have no manners!'"

"'Shame, shame!'"

And we both laugh, though not as hysterically as we did on Tristan.

7. A ROYAL VISIT

Dad was standing in the kitchen looking at the telegram in his hand. I'd heard the radio officer come and I ran to the front door, but Dad was there first.

'What does it say?' Mummy asked. She had just taken some tins of bread out of the oven and she turned them out, upside down on a board, knocking them on the bottom with her knuckle to see if they were baked through.

Dad said 'it's dated 1 January 1957, and it says *'21756 best thanks dukeedinburgh what needed maximum twohundred words pressrated preparations programmes descriptive scene landing 1500 gmt 16/1 upfollowed maximum threehundred pressrated 17/1 dukes activities reception ethighlights generally capturing picture and atmosphere fullstop collect facilities arranged fullstop photos not needed thanks'*

'What does that mean?' I asked inquisitively.

'There's a big international news organisation called Reuters,' he explained. 'They want me to report the visit of the Duke of Edinburgh and this is how they want me to do it.'

I knew of his visit, of course. The whole island was talking about it all the time. 'But why is he coming?' I asked.

'Because this settlement is called the settlement of Edinburgh, after a previous royal visitor who came about a hundred years ago, which is why the Duke wants to come, I expect.'

'Oh! Two Dukes of Edinburgh!'

'That's it.'

Mikey came in, holding a boat he'd been making in Dad's workshop.

'Daddy, I want to paint this boat.'

'That's all right, son. What colour do you want?'

'White, like the island boats. I saw Fardy Sidney painting his boat the other day. And I want stripes round the top.'

'Let's go and see what I've got.'

Preparations for the Duke had been going on for months. The island men had indeed been repainting their wood and canvas longboats, white with red and blue stripes under the gunwales. Then they had started on their houses. Made of island stone and thatched with New Zealand flax which grew in great hedges everywhere on the settlement, the cottages were lined inside with wood. The islanders painted them in reds, greens and blues. Mum didn't like it much. She had chosen pea-green and white for our sitting room, and then she and Dad decided on red and white for the outside of the bungalow.

After a few minutes Dad came back into the house.

'I found some white paint for Michael, and we've got a bit of green left from when we painted the sitting room and red from the outside. He seems well satisfied with those. I'll see you later, Dil. I'm off to the village hall site.'

Mum and Dad were fully involved in all the preparations. Gangs of men had been working on the foundations of the new village hall, including Dad, who loved physical work and took his share in mixing and pouring concrete. The Duke would lay the foundation stone and name the building 'Prince Philip Hall'.

Dad also organised the cleaning of the little church of St Mary, while Mum, recovered from her morning sickness, spring-cleaned our house with the help of three island girls. She would host some of the Britannia's crew to tea, and everything had to be spotless.

I watched her cut the crust off one of the fresh loaves. My mouth watered. She always had the first crust.

'Can I have some?'

'No,' she said, covering it with butter and sinking her teeth into it.

'Why not? It's not fair – you always have the crust!'

'That's because I'm the one who makes the bread.'

We tucked into slices of her fresh loaf for tea, and then went to bed at six o'clock as usual. As the big day drew nearer there was more for our parents to do, and they said they wanted quiet evenings to Get On With Things. One such evening Mum said 'we're going out after supper to the administrator's, children. We won't be far away. You can shout through one of the windows and somebody will hear you if you need us.'

Mikey, Ba and I were used to Mum and Dad going off sometimes in the evening, leaving us on our own, secure in the knowledge that we were perfectly safe. The administrator's house was just above ours on a path which ran the length of the 'station'. We children were in and out of each other's houses all the time and there were no fears when we were left on our own. Ba was usually asleep by the time they went out anyway, and Mikey and I had our comics to read.

My mother's letter tells her parents that this meeting went well. Between them they produced a seating plan for lunch with the Duke, which Pat the administrator and his wife Joy were hosting. This had my mother seated between the Duke on her left and his equerry on her right. Being such a shy person, she was very apprehensive about this. 'I quake when I think of poor little me sitting eating my lunch with the Duke on my left and Michael Parker on my right!!!' says her letter; but then a practical problem claimed her attention.

Joy, the administrator's wife, had ordered special crockery, silver and glassware for the Duke's visit. As happened so often, the ship bringing the supplies had cabled to say that it would no longer be calling at the island, so Joy was in despair. My mother came to the rescue, humorously writing home 'Our new cruet will be used at luncheon, the Duke will stand on our bedroom rugs when he changes his uniform, and he will use one of my small hand-painted tea serviettes when tea is served from the lovely hand-painted tea cloth that the people of St Barnabas gave me when I left!'

She dined out on this story for the rest of her life, amusing herself by selecting various acquaintances known for being somewhat snobbish. 'I shall tell her that Prince Philip wiped his royal lips on this serviette of mine,' she would decide gleefully. 'And then I shall tell her "and do you know, *I haven't washed it since...*"'

She was also exercised over us, her children, about what we would wear and how we should behave, as well as her own outfit. Although she was nearly four months pregnant, her constant sickness had meant that she had lost weight. To her delight the new pink dress she had bought in Cape Town still fitted her. She added a little pink head-hugging hat that was fashionable in the fifties.

'What shall I wear?' I asked her. I always took a great interest in clothes.

'Oh, I should think your bridesmaid's dress again. If it still fits you.'

Although I had grown in height I was thin, and so the dress, with its huge hem, did still fit me. Ba had an identical dress, and we were to wear them with white berets crotcheted by the island women, white gloves and red sandals.

'I hope it'll be hot,' I said. 'I don't want to wear a cardigan over the top – it spoils it.'

'I hope it will be cold,' Mikey said.

'Why?'

'So I can wear my Tristan ganzey.'

'Well, January is summer here,' Mum said. 'It will probably be too warm.'

Mikey started looking mutinous, so she said 'but you can wear your braces instead if you like.'

He beamed. He didn't care much about clothes, but he did want to be like the island boys as much as possible.

I took Ba into the sitting room.

'When you're presented to the Duke, you have to curtsey,' I told her.

'My tarn't turtsey,' she said dubiously.

'I'll show you,' I decided. 'Look, you take your skirt in your hands like this. No! Don't lift it up as high as that! You don't want the Duke to see your pants!'

Ba dropped her skirt. 'My tarn't do it,' she pouted.

'Of course you can!'

She thrust out her head, glared at me and said in a belligerent voice 'My – tarn't – do – it, Gee. So dere!'

I recognised where she got that look and that voice from. It was from Mikey and me when we were arguing. I countered with my mother's don't-make-a-fuss tone.

'Now look at me,' I said persuasively. 'You put one foot behind the other, like this – and then you just bend your knees, like this.'

Eventually she managed to get her feet, her knees, her hands and her skirt all working in the right order. At two-and-a-half she was still a tiny child, pretty with her gold-brown curls and almond-shaped eyes, and she dropped a graceful curtsey. I was satisfied.

'If you do it like that everyone will think how clever you are.'

'My *am* c'ever,' she said earnestly.

'And the Duke,' I said, following up this positive attitude, 'will go home and tell Princess Anne about how little Ba Bell on Tristan da Cunha did the best curtsey he had ever, ever seen in the whole world.'

She beamed, and skipped a bit, and rushed off to show Mummy her turtsey.

Another telegram arrived on 26th January, the day before the Duke's visit. *'31552 further 21756 of 31/12 if duke speaks village hall and school as programme welcome extra twohundred words pressrated direct quotes if possible thanks – reuter'*

Dad was going to have plenty to write.

The days prior to the visit had been very wet, but the seventeenth of January was cloudy and dry. Dad donned his suit and clerical collar and Mum her pink dress and hat. I watched her as she patted her hair into place and picked up her gloves.

'Can we come and see the Duke landing too?'

'No. Children aren't allowed. You'll get your chance at the garden party,' and pulling on her gloves she and Dad went down the wooden steps of the house, across the garden, out of the gate and up the side of our valley towards the beach.

Mikey looked at me. We were still in our old clothes: we would not be presented to the Duke until later.

'We can go and watch him land from the cliff top,' he said. 'Nobody will see us.'

I hesitated. We'd been told to stay at home. 'Don't be silly. Everyone will see us.'

'Mummy and Daddy won't. Then we can run really fast back home and get here before them, and they won't know we've been out.'

Sometimes grownups made unreasonable rules. We left Ba with Harriet, and ran out through the gate.

When we arrived at the cliff top it seemed like the whole island was there. Five of the newly-painted longboats had gone out to meet the ship, and we all stood and watched on the clifftop overlooking the sweep of black sand with the canning factory that was Big Beach. The sun appeared from behind the clouds, setting the sea sparkling, flickering on the bright colours of the women's best clothes. Their headscarves tugged in the breeze.

Mikey was very good at sliding through crowds to the front. I followed rapidly in his wake, anxious not to be left behind, and saw below us at the foot of the cliff a very odd sight: the island men, normally dressed in old clothes for fishing and factory work, were all in their dark Sunday suits and ties. Prince Philip was in clear sight in his longboat coming to shore and somebody exclaimed 'the Duke has the tiller!' One of the station men nearby said 'well, what do you expect – he is an Admiral of the Fleet. He served on destroyers in the navy before his wife became queen. This must be easy for him.'

We listened, and I looked at the Duke's face, and I said to Mikey quietly 'He's doing it because he likes it.'

'Wish I could steer a boat,' he said longingly. We watched on.

As the boat rode the breakers to the beach, the island men grasped the sides to steady it and then hauled it up the beach. The Duke was young, tall and slim with fair hair and beard, and when he jumped easily out of the boat everyone cheered.

I dug Mikey in the ribs. We could see Mum and Dad, with the administrator and his wife, and headwoman Martha Rogers with her husband

Arthur whom everyone called Arfa and Marfa. I watched Mum curtsey and shake hands, and then she followed the Duke and his welcome party into the canning factory.

'Why is he going into the factory?' Mike asked, sitting down on the grass while there was nothing to watch.

I shrugged. 'Dunno. I suppose he wants to see everything. And the factory is important.'

'Why?'

'Because,' I said, rehearsing what I'd been told, 'it's the only way the islanders have of making money. They put the crawfish into tins and send them to South Africa and they get sold there, and the money must come back here.'

Mikey grunted. 'What do they need money for? They have everything they need for free – fish and meat and taters to eat. And they have sheep and spin the wool to make socks and ganzeys. So why do they need money too?'

I knew this. 'Mummy said the diet isn't good enough to keep everyone healthy. We need fruit too, and butter – things like that. And clothes,' I added, mindful that one of my best treats was a new dress from the island canteen or shop.

'They're coming out from the factory,' Mikey said suddenly. 'Quick. Run.'

We raced over the grass, passing the huge wooden arch made for the Duke by the headmaster. It was white, painted with a picture of Tristan with a crown over the top and the words 'Welcome to the Settlement of Edinburgh.'

We were home well before our parents arrived, because they went round the village with the Duke.

110

He only had the one day on Tristan; as a result, his programme was full and carefully recorded by Dad, mindful of his Reuters article. He followed the Duke in to Johnnie and Sophie Green's house to see the women sitting in a row carding wool, their carders with the wire teeth briskly brushing the raw wool into cylinders or rolags. Prince Philip took much more than a cursory interest in the house, Dad wrote later. He asked to see the other rooms (there was only one, their bedroom), then sat in the kitchen to take a stone out of his shoe, chatting easily about their domestic life and how it differed from the past. In Big Herbie and Rachel's house the women were spinning, and then at Fred and Big Mary's the wool was being twisted in preparation for knitting.

The Duke of Edinburgh emerges from an island house, followed by the administrator, Pat Forsyth-Thompson. My father on the right

He examined the display of crafts which had occupied the islanders for months. The main room in Chief Willie Repetto's house hosted a display of model boats and spinning wheels, bullock carts and yokes, polished horns and moccasins. Penguin tassels, from the rockhopper penguins that frequented the seas around the island, had been made into mats. There were also sheepskin mats, baby cradles, a fishing-line made of flax thread and much more. The island women, expert knitters, had produced stockings and pullovers from the wool of the island sheep.

On a separate table were the handmade toys: goose feather boats and whistles, balls and boats made from kelp, and hard marbles made from the dried eyes of the bluefish which were so plentiful in Tristan waters. The royal visitor was to take home a model longboat for the Queen, a cardigan made of undyed brown wool for himself, a model boat and fish-eye marbles for Prince Charles and for Anne, a working model spinning wheel. They all also were to have a pair of island stockings, the sort everyone wore – including us, when the days were chilly. They needed holding up with elastic garters under the knee. Did they end up inside the royal wellingtons as they tramped round their Sandringham estate?

Then it was Dad's big moment. He accompanied the Prince into the church and showed him the organ which had been given to the island by Queen Mary, the white ensign laid up from HMS Magpie on which the Duke had been Commander, and the stone font which had been shipwrecked. He signed the church register, where his signature with the big looping P is proudly preserved to this day.

After visiting old Tom Rogers, who was bed-bound, Prince Philip was taken from the village to the station to meet the expatriates and to have lunch with the Administrator. Mum had left the royal party and come home to supervise scrubbing and dressing us to get us ready to be presented.

'For goodness' sake, stand still, Michael. I'll never get your hair tidy if you don't.'

Mikey stopped fidgeting and did as he was told. He loathed his blonde curls and wanted Mum to flatten his hair as much as possible.

When we were ready to her satisfaction, I grabbed Ba's hand and we climbed our steps to the path above the house which took us to the administrator's garden. We arrived to find it crowded with the station people and their families, but at last it was our turn as we queued up with the other station children to be presented to him.

I curtseyed, and shook him by the hand. Mikey bowed low and did the same. The Duke said 'And how old are you, Michael?'

'Five and three quarters,' said Mikey proudly.

'Good gracious, you are a big chap. I thought you were about seven.'

I could tell Mikey was thrilled. He stayed as near the Duke as he could from then on.

I watched Ba to see what she would do. She managed a little bob curtsey but when the Duke held out his hand to shake hers, she backed off, saying 'no tank-you vewy much!' I shot a glance at our mother. Poor Mummy. I could tell she was hugely embarrassed, but I wasn't sure why, when she knew he had children of about the same age, so he must be used to children being like that. He just seemed to think it was funny and spoke to one of Ba's friends, three-year-old Jane. 'See my Duke's ribbon?' she said, pointing to the one in her hair.

1. We children with the Duke: my sister Ba in the middle, with the beret.

2. My mother in the foreground, as on a recent Tristan stamp.

'Your Duke's ribbon! How splendid,' he said, looking at my mother for an explanation.

'Anything the children have saved for your visit is known as 'the Duke's',' she explained. 'Duke's dresses, duke's shirts, Duke's shoes ….'

He turned to five-year-old Richard, who was hobbling about in new shoes.

'Are those your Duke's shoes?'

'Yes,' said Richard shyly.

'Well, they don't look very comfortable to me,' was the rejoinder.

Mrs Meyer, who had recently had twins, had brought them both, one on each arm. She offered one to the Duke and when he declined everyone laughed. I didn't know why that was funny. There must be certain things a royal visitor just didn't do.

When it was over, we children went home for something to eat with Harriet, and it was time for the lunch my mother was dreading. Instead, 'lunch was not a bit the ordeal I had expected,' she wrote to her parents. 'Prince Philip chatted gaily throughout the meal and Michael Parker, on my right, had one long stream of questions he wanted to ask. He had heard from the doctor that several babies were expected shortly on the station and wanted to know who were the lucky mothers' … followed by six exclamation marks, as my mother then had to make up her mind whether to confess that she was one of them.

After lunch the Prince went to the school to admire a display of our work, and to watch some of us dance. Then it was off to the foundations of the new village hall, where he put a shilling under the foundation stone he laid, and donated his royal standard for the hall. He was taken to see almost everything else: the hospital, the canteen shop, the display of pedigree cattle that the administrative officer had brought out to improve the Tristan breed. Afterwards there was a football match between the island men and the Britannia crew. Honour was satisfied with a two-all draw.

Tea, and a dance for the adults. I had turned eight the previous month and so was allowed to go. Still garbed in my Duke's dress and beret, I followed my parents up to the village and into the half-built hall. The music had already started and I watched as the Duke was given a cushion for the traditional island pillow dance. Normally a girl took a cushion and walked around the hall with it while the music played: she then had to choose a man, and the two would kneel on the cushion and kiss. He would rise from his knees, take the cushion, and then choose a girl. We danced it in children's dances too and I knew what terrible teasing would follow.

I felt the atmosphere of expectancy as everyone waited for the Duke to choose one of the women. Everyone assumed it would be one of the younger ones. The question was, who? I knew this would never be forgotten by the community and so I watched avidly. When he dropped the pillow in front of Pamela Glass, who, with her wavy brown hair and dark eyes was, in my view, the prettiest girl on the island. She went very red but she allowed herself a royal kiss. Then, smiling self-consciously, she walked around the room with the cushion, followed in a line by the Duke and everyone else who had taken part.

The Duke must have enjoyed himself because he gave a six-volt amplifier and three-speed record player to the islanders for their future dances in the new Prince Philip Hall.

Afterwards my mother scurried home with me, to get tea ready for her posh visitors. She had been baking for days. The best china had come out with the best linen, and Harriet and I had arranged the cakes on plates and helped make sandwiches. Mum had ensured everything was immaculate, but she was so put-about that afterwards she couldn't remember anybody's name. Admiral Sir Somebody-or-other, she says vaguely in the letter to her parents. And an Air Force officer. And an elderly man ... they were all very nice indeed, she adds, and the children handed round the food. Very nicely.

I don't remember this event, but we often acted as waiters when my parents had people for meals. It was my mother who taught me how to lay a table, where to put the mats, how to order the cutlery and make sure the glasses were shining. Her best tablecloth was damask, in red and white, with matching napkins, and everything was always carefully laundered.

By 7pm it was pouring with rain, and time for the royal party to go back to the Britannia. Prince Philip borrowed a raincoat, but there weren't enough to go round his party. His equerry ended up wearing Dad's clerical cloak, which caused some royal guffaws. The duke was so taken with it that at one point he stopped everyone and took a photo with a miniature camera: 'that is one we shall never see, I expect' laments my mother in the letter. I'd love to know if it ended up in a royal photo album.

117

The day ended in reverse to its beginning. The duke climbed into a longboat, the island men pushed the boat into the sea, everyone cheered and watched until the boats reached the Britannia. Then they all hurried home out of the rain and my mother, exhausted but pleased and relieved, had an early night.

My father was still awake and up when, later that evening, the radio officer came round with another radio message, this one sent from the Britannia.

'I AM MOST GRATEFUL FOR A PERFECTLY WONDERFUL DAY. NONE OF US WILL EVER FORGET TRISTAN CHEERFULNESS AND HOSPITALITY. WE SEND YOU ALL OUR BEST WISHES FOR A VERY HAPPY FUTURE. PHILIP.

I still have this telegram, and there was a coda for my father. Post Office Telegraphs on the 18th January, the day after the Prince's visit, sent him another:

41802 thanks duke curtainraiser right lines – reuter

Reuters must have been particularly pleased, because my father kept a letter from them dated 21 January, 1957:

'Thank you very much for your reports of the Duke of Edinburgh's visit to Tristan. In content and length these were just what we wanted and our Accounts will be sending you a remittance of £10 which we hope you will accept for this work on our behalf ... '

That's £204 at today's prices. They go on formally to offer him the job of corresponding for them from Tristan in the future, and they enclose three newspaper cuttings made up from his reports. It's signed by their Chief News Editor. It was only later that I discovered that Dad, despite the fact that we had little money, had given all this largesse away to charity.

'You know something?' I say to Mike now. 'I've always assumed, abetted by Mum, that I got my love of reading, writing and words from her. Certainly she was more of a reader than Dad who was remarkably slow, but he was the one who loved writing. In this, as in so many ways, I seem to have ended up with some of his genes.'

'Hmm.' I could see his brain moving into Evidence-Based Thinking. 'I think that although you do/did have a joy in reading and writing, I think it's more to do with the way your brain is wired.'

'Meaning?'

If you can decode the written word fast enough then reading can be effortless and a joy. If, like me, it's all a bit of an effort and, even when you do succeed, the story is less interesting than reality, you soon give up.

'I'm not sure I've ever fully realised before how much of a chore reading was for you. You've always been such a scientific cleverclogs and it's obscured that tendency.'

Mike gave his thinking-about-it sniff.

'Clearly these tendencies are inherited genetically to a significant degree.'

Well, I don't know.

8. OUR BABY BROTHER

At 7am on the morning of 26 June 1957, my mother waddled into the bedroom I shared with Mikey and woke us. I sat up, looking blearily at her in her long seersucker cotton dressing gown with the little red and white squares. She had it done up over her bump, as she called it.

'Children, get up at once. Get dressed quickly as you can.' She waved her hand fast and jerkily, like she did when she wanted us to respond urgently.

'Why?' I said.

'The baby's coming.'

I yelped, slid out of bed and raced Mikey to the bathroom. We skimped on our cold washes, reckoning our mother would not be checking on us. Then I got Lizzie dressed.

'You're going to the administrator's for breakfast,' Mum said. 'They'll look after you.'

'When can we come back?'

'When the baby's arrived. I'll send Harriet to call you. It should be here by lunchtime.'

'Come on children, at once,' said my father who had already been up to the administrator's wife and asked her to have three extra children for breakfast. We ended up there quite often – their house was the nearest to ours. Mikey played with their son Patrick, and Margaret was about four and played with Lizzie who was now three. They spoke in a certain way, and Margaret couldn't pronounce her own name then. Behind their backs we called them Partrick and Gargie.

With us out of the way, my mother and Harriet set to work to prepare the bedroom. They put a rubber drawsheet under the bottom sheet. They got out clean towels. My mother put the baby clothes in a neat pile: she had been knitting and sewing for months. The big wooden cradle was made up with baby blankets and sheets. Harriet pumped up the primus stove in the kitchenette and put water on to boil. My father went to fetch the doctor and the nurse.

Dr Gooch examined my mother and pronounced everything fine. It was 8.30am and he judged the baby would arrive about 9.45am. He went home for his breakfast. Sister Brent stayed with her and gave her an injection of Pethidin, and she went back to sleep.

Just before 10am my mother woke. By this time the doctor had returned and she said at once 'I need to push!'

He laughed.

'No, not yet,' he said. 'Having that injection slowed you down. It will be another hour at least,' and he and my father went into the living room to discuss school business.

My mother, half sitting-up, said suddenly to Sister Brent 'He's wrong, you know. I badly need to push this minute.'

'Let me take a look,' said Nurse Brent, who was unflappable.

'It's coming now ...' announced my mother as the nurse caught sight of the baby's head crowning.

121

By the time Dr Gooch and my father had crossed the kitchen from the living room into the bedroom, Christopher Francis Tristan, a big healthy boy, was already born and roaring loudly.

My parents were thrilled. They had hoped for a second son to keep Mikey company and had chosen names long since. He was 8lbs 12oz, a big baby for my tiny mother, and she needed numerous stitches. She did not mind after such a fast and easy labour. Christopher was washed and dressed, yelling all the time, and put to the breast. The room was tidied up and Harriet made tea for my thirsty mother.

The first we knew was when we were playing with Partrick and Gargie on our favourite rock, a big grey wedge-shaped boulder with a flat top that we called the ship rock. I was sitting astride when I saw Harriet crest the side of the little valley in which we lived. She walked quickly towards us, her cotton skirt and short, straight dark hair blown by the wind.

'You-all can come home,' she said when she was within earshot.

'What is it?' I asked eagerly.

'You'se got a baby brother.'

'Supersonic!' I yelled and raced home, followed closely by Mikey while Harriet brought Lizzie. I arrived breathless in my mother's bedroom to find her sitting up in bed looking just the same as usual, with a bundle wrapped in a white baby blanket in her arms.

'Come and see your new baby brother,' she said, smiling, knowing how excited I was and how much I loved babies.

122

'Careful,' warned Sister Brent. 'Don't bounce on the bed.'

I calmed down and hung over the baby while my mother teased the folds of blanket away from his face. 'He's wonderful ...' I breathed.

'Michael,' said our mother. 'You wanted a baby brother and here he is. Meet Christopher.'

Mikey took a cursory glance at the baby.

'Hmph!' he announced. 'He looks like a red-faced tomato,' and after a few minutes he went off to do something more interesting. I was rather shocked. I thought he should be more impressed, or at least realise that this was a very special event and that he should behave accordingly. But he had a point. The baby's face was dark pink and all squashed together, and so fat he could hardly open his eyes. But my mother only laughed, and helped Lizzie climb on the bed. She put her face down on the baby and patted him gently.

That same day my father took a piece of lined foolscap paper and wrote 'Father and Mrs Bell are very happy to announce the birth of their second son on Wednesday June 26th at 10 o'clock. He weighed 8 lbs 12 oz and will be named Christopher Francis Tristan'. He signed it with the date, put on his black mackintosh as it had started to rain, and made his way up the muddy track to the church notice board. Dodging the boys who were driving family donkeys to their tethers, he opened the notice board window and pinned up his announcement. Somebody – I don't know who - had gone with him and captured it all on cine film. He kept that notice all his life, and it is now in my brother's possession, still with the drawing-pin marks in it.

His next stop was the radio hut, where he sent a telegram to his parents to announce Christopher's birth. He added 'STRIKINGLY LIKE MICHAEL DILYS AND BABY EXTREMELY WELL. ALL TREMENDOUSLY THRILLED. HEARTFELT THANKS GODS BLESSING YOUR PRAYERS. LOVE. PLEASE PHONE THIS MESSAGE TO BARROW. PHILIP.'

Barrow in Furness was where my mother's parents lived.

Dad spent the rest of the day washing the sheets soiled by the birth in cold water. I have no idea why. It was easy to light the geyser with sticks of wood to produce hot water, and they had employed Bartha specially to do the washing. Perhaps it was just that, after all the excitement, he needed something practical to do.

Life settled down. Christopher was a very easy baby who slept all night and fed hungrily during the day. There was no characteristic dip in his birth weight, and a week later my mother wrote that he now exceeded 9 lbs. She was in seventh heaven. Ever since she had been a little girl, she had had an exceptional and instinctive understanding of babies and small children, and would never be happier than when she was with them. Two extra girls were employed to help Harriet, so she was able to rest properly after the birth. She needed to stay in bed for a few days while dealing with strong after-pains, but recovered very quickly. She was full of milk; it would spray out of her nipple all over the baby's face, too fast for him to take it in his mouth first. Her blouses were constantly wet with milk, and when she slept on her front, she would wake up to find two large wet milky Patches on the bottom sheet. Christopher grew and thrived, a weighty and contented baby.

The following month he was christened in a ceremony where Mikey was a server and held the candle, while my father baptised the baby. There was a bevy of godparents, six from the island community, three muddishes (godmothers) and three fardies (godfathers). Another godfather was Roy Cowdry, one-time chaplain to the Archbishop when we lived in Cape Town and who had become a good friend. He was now Bishop of Johannesburg. He cabled *'PRAYERS AND BLESSINGS FOR CHRISTOPHER FRANCIS LOVE TO YOU ALL COWDRY'.*

The islanders were delighted, not only that my parents had had a baby on the island, which made him theirs too, but also that they had included the name Tristan. My mother began receiving gifts from her numerous, characteristically generous visitors who had knitted or sewn caps, bootees, nighties, jackets and mittens. One of Christopher's fardies had made him a big wooden rocking cradle, and before the birth we had all worked with our father to sand it down and paint it. I loved it, and spent hours rocking Christy to sleep with my foot on a rocker while I read a book at the same time. My parents had also managed to get a new spring for our high pram which had been shipped out with us. Christy was put to sleep outside in the garden whenever it was sunny.

My mother recovered so rapidly that she was back teaching in the school only a month after the birth. As for me, I was in a state of bliss. I had a baby brother whom I could cuddle whenever I liked. I rapidly learned to change him, wash him, put on his nappy – being careful with that big safety-pin – and dress him. My mother expected responsibility from me and I gave it to her. I watched him and played with him and took him outside to sit on my knee, and I made him wave his little fat arm to anyone who arrived.

At night, after he graduated from the rocking cradle to Ba's old cot, he did not always settle quickly and we discovered that he liked being patted. I spent evening after evening sitting on the floor by his cot with my arm through the bars, patting his bottom while he lay on his tummy. I got a bit bored in the end, so fetched a copy of Hymns Ancient and Modern, and sang my way through them until he was asleep. I remember the last number was 779. I was teaching myself to play the piano which was in the house, and I was learning to read music, so if I didn't know a tune, I would go into the living room during the day and pick out the melody on the piano. I have a feeling that I wasn't always accurate, but Christy wasn't fussy. He always went to sleep in the end.

Unknown to me, my mother mourned over the fact that my father's mother, who preferred Mikey and Ba, had sent them more presents for Christmas than for me. She decided to make it up to me, so, somehow, she managed to order me a new doll. I adored dolls and played with them constantly, but the new one was something very special. On 3rd February 1958, a few weeks after my ninth birthday, I dipped my nib pen in the bottle of ink and wrote to my mother's mother:

'I must tell you about a beautiful, beautiful present that Mummy and Daddy gave me for my birthday. It arrived just a little later, in January. I was practising 'Girls and Boys come out to Play' (on the piano) when, suddenly, the door opened, and in came Mummy and Daddy, Mummy with a big red box covered with pretty black and white pictures. "Gilly," she said, 'This is a very special present for you, because you have been so good and so helpful to me for a long time, especially with Christopher." She set the box down on the chair behind me. I lept up, and opened the box. There, lying on its back, was a beautiful doll. (Baby.) Rooted, golden hair glinted and shone in the sunshine, half shut shining blue eyes stared up, pretty deep red lips where like peoples. A lovely white, green spotted dress with a full skirt and a bonnet to match was on her, lacey panties, pretty socks and white bowed shoes were the rest of the clothing. She was really beautiful. I called her Judith. Goodbye for now. Lots of love Gillian xxxxxxxxx'

Poor old Judith. She's lost one of those sparkling blue eyes, and is rather worse for wear, but she still wears that green spotted dress. It's been mended a time or two.

'You really weren't the slightest bit interested at first in that baby, were you?' I announce to Mike.

'Nope. Babies weren't interesting. That was girls' stuff.'

'We would call that a sexist attitude these days – although it was perfectly acceptable then.'

'It was more that I lived on my own planet – I got on with the things that interested me.'

'Very focused! – but this baby was your little brother – don't you remember feeling pleased that it was a boy and not another girl?'

'I suppose I must have been,' he says vaguely. I try another tack.

'Do you think that having a baby brother, who took up so much of everyone's time – Mum breastfeeding him, Harriet adoring him as her godson, Lars and Sidney, his fardies, coming to the house to see him – made you feel left out or less loved?'

'Don't think so. You know how it was with us. We were very accepting of things that came along.'

'It was the fifties – children may have had opinions but there was no way they were ever going to trump what parents wanted. Wonder if we've all gone too much the other way? Parents giving in to children, getting them what they want, not wanting to tell them that they can't have things?'

'That never happened with us. Mum and Dad were quite strict and it was always clear what was expected of us.'

'Not that we always did it ...'

9. PLANTING IN

'I don't want to go to the potato Patches again,' I wailed. 'We went yesterday! Why do we have to go again today?' I loathed going. I loathed gardening. It was always so tedious, and there was always so much of it, and it was so mucky, and we had to do it over and over again, and the dirt and the soil and the manure would get into the eczema on my hands. I had to wash them and wash them with soap and it made the eczema worse than ever.

There was no sympathy from my father.

'Because it's a lovely day and the islanders are all going out to do their planting in, and we're going to help,' he said firmly. 'We have to grow our own food here in order to give you all a healthy diet. Everyone has to help. He who will not work,' he added, quoting St Paul as he usually did, 'let him not eat.'

I hated it when he said that. It was always so final. He had been given his own patch by the islanders so it would be a long and boring day, not only working in our own patch but helping with others as well.

'I hate going! And anyway, we had to walk yesterday, and today my legs are aching.' I hoped this sally would sway my softer-hearted mother into taking my side, but Mikey intervened instead.

'That's 'coz girls aren't as strong as boys,' he said smugly. 'My legs aren't aching the tiniest bit.'

'Boys are not stronger than girls,' I said angrily, aware nonetheless that I had taken the bait and was heading for my own downfall in this argument.

'Well in that case there's no good reason why you shouldn't go,' said my mother inevitably. 'I'll come out later with Ba and bring you a picnic.'

I stamped my foot and pouted. This was not enough to offset the boredom at the Patches. I tried another tack.

'Well – can I ride on a donkey?' I enquired hopefully. 'Can I ride White Fake?' This jinny belonged to Michael Repetto and his wife Olive and he used to lend her to us sometimes. Riding her would make up for a great deal that I disliked.

Women riding sidesaddle to the Patches

'No,' said my father. 'You're young and strong and you can walk.'

'It's such a long way!' I objected furiously.

'It's less than 4 miles.'

'That's a very long way especially as we did it yesterday! And why can't I ride White Fake?'

'Because Michael Repetto needs her to carry his sacks of seed potatoes.'

'I hate going to the Patches!' I yelled, and flung outside, slamming the door on purpose.

My parents as usual took no notice of my tantrum and within a few minutes my father, with some provisions in his knapsack on his back, was walking north along the track out of the village. I went grumpily one side of him, Mikey cheerfully on the other. He liked gardening, and he didn't mind walking, and he liked doing what the island boys did, who would be there with their families. Resigned now to my lot, I started checking off the landmarks. First came Hottentot Gulch, then Hillpiece which meant that we were getting nearer and so there was less far to walk.

There was another reason I disliked walking to the Patches with Daddy. Because for us it was a long walk, he took the opportunity to talk to us about our 'bodies,' and it was no different today.

'The trouble is,' he was saying, as he often said, 'that my parents and grandparents thought that bodies were rather rude and that we should keep them covered up. So I grew up thinking there was something wrong with us. Mummy and I don't want you to get like that.'

'We're not like that,' I argued, trying to head him off. 'We don't think bodies are rude, Daddy.'

'I'm very glad to hear it,' he said, but continued imperturbably. 'You see, God created our bodies, and what God creates is good. This is why Mummy and I like you to have baths together and not to worry about being in your birthday suits. I grew up in a boys' boarding school and I had no idea what

131

girls looked like until I was married. That isn't healthy.'

'I know' I said impatiently. 'You always tell us that.' I decided to be more blunt. 'Daddy, why do you always talk to us about this when we walk to the Patches?'

'Because it's a good time – we're together and nothing interrupts us.'

'But you keep on talking about it. And I don't really like it. And –' I shot a warning look at Mikey - 'Mikey doesn't either.'

'Why not?' said my father, plainly troubled by this admission, which he suspected betrayed exactly the attitude he was deploring.

It's ... it's ...' I searched for the right word 'It's embarrassing.'

'Oh!' said my father, his suspicions confirmed. 'And do you think the same as Gilly, Mike?'

'A bit,' said Mikey cautiously, not wanting to give our father the opportunity for an extended explanation as to why such an attitude was wrong.

'You shouldn't be embarrassed,' he said in the sort of voice he always used when he had decided to keep going with the topic under discussion. 'That's exactly what Mummy and I are trying to teach you. There's nothing to be embarrassed about. Bodies are perfectly natural and normal and that's the way we should look at them.'

I heaved a sigh, and gave up, but I was not convinced. The island children thought bodies were hilarious and were always making jokes that discomfited me. I wanted to be left alone, and only talk about it when I wanted to, but there was no chance of that in our family.

As we arrived at the Patches many island families were already hard at work, having begun at daybreak.

Potato Patches (byGosh.com)

'There's Fardy Sidney!' said Mikey happily. Sidney was Christy's godfather and he and Alice's house was our second home. They were the nearest thing we had to an uncle and aunt on the island. Their daughters Pammy and Trina were there too, together with other members of the family. Sidney looked up and grinned at us, his teeth very white in his tanned face, as we went inside the low drystone wall that surrounded each patch.

'Mornin' Faather!' said Sidney. 'You-all done come to do plantin'-in?'

'We certainly have,' said Daddy, running his expert gardener's eye over the work. He didn't always approve of the way the islanders did their gardening, but tended to keep his own counsel, preferring instead to develop a school garden with the boys in the senior class so that he could teach them how to do it in the way he thought was best. But he had reckoned without their slapstick sense of humour. One day he explained what a spit was, and they laughed so much that he got very little work out of them for the rest of that lesson.

'You-all ignore them chance taters,' said Sidney. They were the little spuds left over from digging last autumn which were sprouting up all over the place. There was no time to waste: the islanders always worked at speed in the Patches, and Sidney was already stretching the string out straight and pegging it down to mark the route of the next drill. He and Godfrey began digging the trench, followed by Alice and Trina who put the seed potatoes in pairs, in parallel rows within the trench.

In every patch stood a number of 44-gallon oil drums full of crawfish offal and penguin guano. A pile of offal had been tipped out on the ground from one drum near the patch entrance, and Clement had already filled the bus or wheelbarrow with it. He brought it over to us. Pammy, Mikey and I began to take handfuls of it and I tried not to breathe in, it stank so much. We covered each potato with it. My father and Joseph worked behind us, piling the mould or earth over the top. By the time we were halfway down the drill, Sidney and Godfrey had already started digging the next. Nobody stopped until the whole patch was finished.

I lifted one of my hands tentatively to my nose and sniffed. 'It smells absolutely horrible,' I announced, but they all just laughed at me. We went on to our own patch where Daddy was able to cultivate not just potatoes, but all sorts of vegetables, much more to his own liking.

'First of all,' he said, explaining everything carefully as he always did, 'do you see how the earth is much deeper at one end of the patch than the other? We're going to dig some of it out of the deeper end and transfer it to the shallow end, so that there's a good depth of earth everywhere.'

Mikey surveyed the ground critically. 'Why?' he said. 'Things grow just as well in the shallow end.'

'Because they will grow even better if we give them more room for their roots.'

'I don't see why,' grumbled Mikey, but he went off to fetch the bus because he liked doing that.

After a couple of hours more of hard work I looked up.

'There's Mummy and Ba on a donkey - and it's White Fake!' I dropped my trowel and rushed out of the patch, careful to slow down as I approached so as not to scare the jinny. My mother was riding side-saddle with Ba in front, while Olive, Michael's wife, steadied their donkey with its halter. My mother handed Ba down to me and then slid to the ground.

'Where's Christy?' I asked.

'He's too little to come. I left him at home with his muddish, Granny Mary.'

'How did you come on White Fake? I thought Michael Repetto needed her for carrying potatoes!'

'He did,' said my mother, opening the bag with the picnic. 'Then he sent her back, so that Olive and I could come out with the food.'

Other women and girls were arriving now, some walking and knitting, others riding and knitting, the donkeys carrying cans of food which they had prepared at home. They started to get the lunchtime meal ready for the Patches workers. I flopped down next to Ba, tired and very pleased to stop.

'Pooh,' said Ba pertly. 'Gilly is smelly.'

My father used a drum to store rainwater, and we dipped the rusty liquid out with a bucket and washed our hands as best we could while my mother unpacked hardboiled eggs and Marmite sandwiches. My favourite.

I bit into my egg contentedly and then examined it. I hadn't reached the yolk yet so I took a mouthful of sandwich, as I wasn't keen on the white of egg. The sun was shining and a good breeze blew through our hair. The donkey cropped the grass peacefully just outside the patch wall. I looked out over the blue sea, ruffled with white caps of foam. The air was so clear we could easily see Inaccessible Island. The only thing I disliked now was the stink of rotten offal. I could still smell it on my hands.

After lunch we started again, my father double-digging and putting a layer of manure into the trench before planting. This time I was given the job of cutting the seed potatoes in half and removing some of the shoots. This was much more to my liking and Ba spent her time either making piles of the potatoes, or taking them two by two to Daddy, or sticking them in the ground when nobody was looking. Finally, I got to the bottom of the heap, my father planted and covered the last few, then looked around the patch, with its neat rows of furrows.

'A good day's work, I think,' he said, coming out of the patch and starting to clean off his fork. We tidied up, but I had my eye on the donkey.

'Please can I ride her?'

'For a little while,' said my mother, wiping Ba's hands as best she could. 'Then it's my turn.'

'Super-duper!' It was always a problem getting up on the donkey as the saddle was only a rough seat. There were no reins, bit, bridle or stirrups, just the rope halter. Michael Repetto heaved me up so I could sit side-saddle, and then Mikey was put on astride behind me, riding like the other boys. I took the stick, clicked my tongue, and White Fake moved off.

We made our ponderous way out of the Patches and along the track, with everyone else going home at the same time. The donkeys were loaded with people, food cans and some sacks of guano for the cottage gardens. Ba could not walk fast so eventually Mikey slid off and she came up in front of me for a while. Then she decided that she wanted to run, so she got down and I carried on, delighted to be on my own. We reached Hottentot Gulch and started down the stony ravine side.

Halfway down something startled the donkey and she lurched. I lost my balance and slipped half-off the saddle. I clutched at White Fake's mane but couldn't right myself again, and all around me I could hear people laughing at me. I needed to save face so I took a quick decision. The ground was close, after all. I let go and slid to the ground, landing on my side.

'You fell off, you fell off,' chanted Mikey triumphantly.

I jumped up and brushed down my hands. 'Doesn't matter. It didn't hurt me at all,' I said crossly, ashamed of being the butt of people's amusement.

'That's enough now, children,' said my mother, heading off the impending argument. 'I'm going to ride the rest of the way. I'm an old lady and I'm feeling tired!'

Everyone laughed again at the thought of our lively young mother being old. It was much more fun after that, walking home in a big group, the donkeys nodding their heads, the women knitting, the boys teasing each other and vying with each other to see how far they could throw a stone, the girls knitting too like their mothers and grandmothers. I remembered I had a jumper at home I was knitting for Christy. I'll do some more of that after tea and bath, when I get into bed, I thought.

But later that evening, tucked up under the blanket, after a few rows my eyelids felt heavy. I stuck the needles in the wool and put the knitting on the floor, and looked over at the other bed. Mikey was asleep already, sprawled out on his back. I blew out the candle and lay down on my side, tucking my hands up near my face.

Even after a warm bath and lots of soap, I could still smell that offal.

'I remember now looking at the islanders' Patches,' says my brother, 'and seeing that the earth was piled at one end halfway up the wall, and noticing that the potatoes in the shallow end of the patch grew just as well as the deep end.'

'You accepted it then but clearly your rebel soul was taking shape!'

'I got fed up with it. Dad took me and Hedbit out one day and we spent almost the whole day redistributing the earth in our patch. I thought then it was a complete waste of time, and I still do. It was all of a piece with my realising that grown-ups weren't always right. Dad wasn't always right.'

'And we were bred in those days to think that adults, especially parents, were always right – and we were always being told not to argue with them. Being sent to our rooms, or sent to bed early, as a punishment for arguing.'

'We've brought up our own children differently!'

'It's a whole new subject, which way of parenting was better, and why.'

'I do remember the donkey running away with me one day,' he adds suddenly.

I don't recall this. 'What happened?'

'We were coming home from the Patches, and I was on the donkey, and when we got near the settlement it could see its home, and suddenly bolted. I clung on for dear life, but I was scared witless.'

'That's much more exciting than my gentle slide to the ground,' I say regretfully.

There was always so much possibility on Tristan for an adventure.

10. THE LOST BOATS

A faint sound was waking me up. I rolled on to my back and listened. It was the gong, the empty metal cylinder hung from a wooden frame on the island. When the weather was fine enough for the island men to go fishing, somebody always hit the gong at 6am.

It was overlaid with another sound, like the deep boom from the biggest organ pipe. I knew that noise well. It was a whale blowing and we would often see them, some with calves, swimming up and down out to sea.

I dozed off again for a while, then came to with a jerk, scrambled out of bed and padded outside on to the veranda. There they were, as I knew they would be.

The sea was glassy blue and smooth, the air so still and clear that I could hear the chugging of the white motorboat as it came round the headland into sight on my right. Behind it, towed in a long straight line, were the black fishing dinghies. The motorboat would take them to the fishing grounds, where they would drop their rock lobster pots into the water, leaving only the round cork floats bobbing on the surface. The men would spend all day fishing, and then they would collect up the pots, and the fish they had caught with rod and line. The motorboat would reappear, and late in the afternoon we would see them coming back again, towed to Big Beach where the catch would be landed and taken to the canning factory there.

Canning factory on Big Beach with dinghies at the front. This would all be covered by lava from the 1961 volcano which flared at Pigbite, in the distance

I never tired of the sight of the long line of black dinghies on the calm blue water. I waited until they had disappeared round the next headland, then went to get washed and dressed.

The weather governed our life on Tristan completely. South Atlantic storms were so violent they tore the roofs off some of the houses and scattered wooden huts, smashing them into fragments. We weren't allowed outside and the school was closed. It wasn't safe with metal and wood flying around.

Rough weather had a major effect on us. We had to endure seeing ships sail away without taking our precious bags of mail on board, because the sea was too wild. We had to wait for the right weather before we could go out to the potato Patches, to

141

spade and put in, or to have the day off to go ratting, or sail round the island to the orchards at Sandy Point. The fishermen had to wait for the right weather to go fishing or to Nightingale Island, 30 miles away.

I knew by now that the islanders were experts on the state of the sea. They could read all the moods of the sea like a book, and usually knew what would and would not be possible with the boats. They built their boats themselves, stretching canvas tightly over wooden ribs, painting it white and blue with stripes of red under the gunwales. They made oars and masts and tillers, mainsails and jib sails. The boats were like relatives: they each had a traditional family name. Nobody needlessly risked such a valuable possession. But our weather was always unpredictable, changing sometimes very fast from fair to stormy.

Every year over a hundred islanders would set off in the boats to sail to Nightingale Island for a fatting trip. Nightingale was overrun with nesting penguins and sea birds. It was inhospitable to humans with its jungle of tussock, but the islanders prized the penguin guano to bring back for their Patches. They took empty sacks with them, and returned with them bulging with the smelly stuff. They also caught some of the sea birds and rendered their fat down to make oil for cooking. We needed fatting trips for our diet.

Nightingale, with kind permission
www.tristandc.com

One day at the end of the summer in March, 1958, the men decided that the wind was in the right direction and the sea was fair enough for eight sailing boats to set off for Nightingale on the annual fatting trip. We went down to the beach to see them off, then we climbed back up to the cliff top and watched them row out to sea and put up their white sails. 'They'se pynting for the hisland,' said the women around us. As they went, we waved and as usual gave three cheers. The voices of the crews came over the water to us as they responded. Then the sails filled and billowed, the boats were soon out of sight and we went home.

It was only much later that I discovered the details of what happened next. On Saturday the men on Nightingale decided to set off home for Tristan. Some of them were doubtful about the weather, but in the end the boats all put out to sea about midday, which was later than they usually started. At first the weather was fair and the boats bowled along under sail, but during the afternoon the weather changed abruptly, as it so often did. The wind shifted direction, the sea made up, and they decided to sail along the east side of Tristan in the lee of the island, rather than the normal west side.

Everyone was always anxious, waiting for the boats. You could never be sure of people's safety on the ocean. Then early on Sunday morning six of the boats appeared, the sails reefed, the oarsmen rowing hard against a strong wind towards Big Beach. Dad went down with the families to welcome them and hear the news.

He came back at breakfast time. As it was Sunday and Harriet had the day off, Mummy was ladling porridge into our bowls as we sat round the table. Harriet's mother had given us some fresh milk from their cow, and we were pouring it carefully on the porridge – not too much, fresh milk was scarce and therefore precious.

'Pass me the Goue Stroop please,' I said to Mikey. Our golden syrup came from South Africa with an Africaans label on the tin and we liked saying the strange words. He handed it to me and I looked at it critically: the spoon with the hole in it was hooked on to the inside of the tin, but the handle was sticky. 'Ergh,' I said. 'You dipped it in too far.'

'No I didn't,' mumbled Mikey, his mouth full of porridge.

'No he didn't,' piped up Ba, who nearly always took his side.

'Stop arguing,' said my mother as she spooned Farex into Christy's mouth. She looked up as my father came in. 'All well?' she asked, putting another spoonful of cereal into Christy's mouth.

'Actually, no,' said my father, taking his place and shaking out his napkin. We all paused and looked at him.

'Why not?' said my mother, wiping Christy's mouth. 'What's the problem?'

'Only six boats have come back.'

Mikey and I stared, our squabble forgotten. We knew eight boats had gone.

'Where are the other two?' I asked.

'Nobody knows,' said Dad. 'I need to eat this quickly and go and find out what I can.'

'But what happened?' Mikey said.

'It seems they were blown out to sea.'

'Why? They always sail together.'

'Nobody's sure,' Dad said again. 'By the time darkness fell last night the boats were in the lee of the island and tied up to the kelp. In the night they didn't realise that two of the boats had gone – probably the kelp tore away so the boats began to drift. The wind most likely blew them out to sea, and it seems that the crews didn't carry a torch, so they couldn't even signal at night when it was happening. One of the boats, the Britannia, only has four men in it, and they usually have five or six. What's more, Victor, who's part of that crew was ill on the morning the boats left Nightingale, and Morris gets terribly sea-sick. The other boat, British Trader, has some very experienced seamen in it but the main worry is that little Jennifer is with them.'

'Jennifer Rogers?' I said, astonished. 'Who's in my class at school? She's only 14!'

'That's right,' said Dad. 'You can imagine how worried her poor family is.'

Nobody thought about anything else all day. My parents visited the islanders continually and sometimes we went with them. Some of the younger men were sent to climb the mountain base and work their way through the difficult terrain to the other side of the island, to see if the boats were there. Most of the islanders stood by the gable ends of their houses, their eyes constantly searching the sea. Normally my parents would be invited inside and offered tea, but nobody thought of that. Instead, one after another told us of a previous time, when almost the whole male population of the island had been lost at sea. Then they were silent. There was little my parents could say.

By Sunday evening there was still no news, and Dad ditched the harvest festival that was scheduled for that night. As he visited, he told the islanders there would be a service of prayer for the lost boats instead.

We went up to the church together after tea. The place was packed, everyone sitting quietly. I looked round at their faces, the women wearing their headscarves, the girls in their berets like mine, the men bareheaded, all their faces solemn. Seeing them like that gave me a heavy feeling. I sat next to my mother, very conscious of the leaden atmosphere. My father began Evensong and as we sang 'Eternal Father, strong to save, whose arm hath bound the restless wave' there was a lot of crying and sniffing all round us. I felt terrible. I wasn't used to grownups crying.

Processing from the church

We went home and Mum put us all to bed, but I could tell she was distracted, and in our family prayers that night we prayed again for the lost boats.

'I don't suppose the families will get much sleep tonight,' she said. 'How worried they must be.'

My father came in just as we were finishing. 'The young men are back,' he said. 'There's no sign of the boats on the other side of the island. And I've been to the radio hut. The radio officer is signalling any shipping in the area, asking them to help in the search.'

I lay awake for a while thinking about Jennifer. I wondered how she felt, in the open boat with the five men, maybe drifting, completely lost. Was she frightened? Was she lying down in the boat, looking up at the sky, wondering if she would ever reach home? I went to sleep thinking about her.

When we woke on Monday morning Dad had already been out early, and there was still no news. 'I'm going to hold a Communion service each morning, and a service of prayer every evening' he was telling the islanders. 'We need the special strength and grace that our Lord gives us in Communion,' and at 7am the church was crowded.

By this time a tanker happened to be in the area, the Camilla, and she had picked up the frantic radio signals and radioed back saying that she would help.

'That's good,' said Mikey when we heard.

'The factory manager has gone out to her in the motorboat,' said my father. 'He's gone with Chief Willie Repetto.'

'Why?' I asked.

'So they can help the captain direct the search.'

We went outside like everyone else, and climbed up the side of our little valley. We saw our regular small fishing ships, the Frances Repetto and the *Tristania*, sailing past the island.

'Everybody's helping as much as they can,' I told Mikey.

'They've come back from Gough Island.'

'How do you know?'

'I heard somebody say so. I think they might be better than the Camilla.'

'Because they know the sea round here much better, you mean.' For once, he and I agreed.

By Monday evening the ships had found no wreckage, no sign, nothing. At 7pm the church was full again. Dad did not use the pulpit, but stood in his cassock and surplice at the front of the church.

There was a hush that was almost breathless, as if everyone was waiting to hear something special.

Dad spoke very simply. He reminded us that Jesus had friends who were fishermen. He recounted the story of the storm on the lake, and the presence of Jesus with the disciples, and his power over the wind and the waves. He explained that this meant Jesus was always with us, even when the seas were rough and his people were frightened. When he finished, I heard a long sigh, as if the whole congregation breathed together.

I stood with him at the door as the islanders filed out. Granny Mary came by, her brown weatherbeaten face framed by her headscarf, her black eyes wise. 'Hi allus say, Father,' she told Dad, 'that hour loved ones his safe in the harms of Jesus whether they's alive or whether they's pass on. We can jus' pray and trust in God.'

I glanced up to see what Daddy would say. 'I couldn't agree more,' he said. It seemed to me that although they had not done so visibly, somehow they had reached out and hugged one other. She gave him a firm nod, and went down the church path.

When we got home it was past our usual bedtime and my mother hurried the others into bed. I helped get Christy ready, so she let me sit up for a little while. When Daddy came in, I was allowed a small cup of Ovaltine – a treat, because it was expensive.

'Why did she say that?' I asked, still mulling over the exchange with Granny Mary.

'Who say what?' said my father, who was tired.

'That they are safe in the arms of Jesus, whether they're alive or dead – that sounds as if it doesn't matter what's happened to them. But it does matter, and everyone knows that.'

My father looked at me and raised his eyebrows. 'My hat!' he exclaimed. 'What thoughts do go round in your busy head!'

'But why?' I persisted. I knew I was about to be sent to bed and I wanted an answer before I went.

'They just think,' he said slowly, 'that God has planned the day of death of each one of us. So it makes no difference whether we're in bed when we die, or in a boat.'

'But they care,' I insisted, thinking of the grave faces in church, the people standing at the gable ends of the houses, endlessly scanning the sea.

'I think they're very sad,' said Dad. 'It will be a terrible thing if they never come back. By the way,' he added to Mum, 'I've had a telegram from the Assistant Bishop of Capetown, Roy Cowdry.'

My mother saw me listening. 'Gilly – that's enough. Go to bed now. Go on. At once.'

I went slowly, and did not quite close the sitting room door. They didn't notice.

'What does he say?' I heard her ask.

'He's distressed to hear of the tragedy. He wants us to convey his heartfelt sympathy to the bereaved.' I saw my father lift the telegram in order to recall the exact wording. 'May God give you all comfort and courage,' he says.'

'They are not dead yet,' said my mother practically. 'Come on, you're exhausted. Let me make some more Ovaltine and then we must get some sleep.'

I pulled the door almost to, so that it would not click, and went to bed. Again I thought about Jennifer. She was only fourteen. Was she dead or alive? Was she scared of dying? How do people on boats die? Supposing they were all dead? Would they ever be found? And if they weren't found, would their boat just drift and drift for ever with their bodies in it? For once, my imagination failed me and my heart beat hard with fear.

At 7am the next day, Tuesday, the church was packed again for Communion, and there was still no news. By this time the boats had been lost for 3 days, without proper rations or enough drinking water. When I found that out, I wondered if they had run out completely, and what Jennifer might be eating. I knew people couldn't drink sea water. Was she thirsty and hungry? And if they couldn't eat or drink, they would get very weak – maybe too weak to steer the boat. When I said my own prayers, I prayed for her most of all.

Radio messages went back and forth to the searching ships, but they found nothing. The islanders still stood at the gable-ends of their cottages, still continually searching the sea. My parents went on visiting them, especially the families of those who were missing.

School had been suspended – nobody could concentrate on anything else. Mikey and I took Ba up the side of our valley, and we played a bit of cricket. Every so often we too would look at the ocean, straining to see anything. I thought how marvellous it would be if I could be the first person to see a lost boat. Even more marvellous for Jennifer if at last she saw Tristan again, and then she would know that she was nearly home. But the sea was empty.

When my father came in mid-afternoon, we were back in the house. Mikey had gone into the shed to make something mysterious with wood, hammer and nails as he often did. Ba and Christy were having their afternoon naps. I had taken out the big box of paints I had been sent by a relative for my birthday, and was painting a sea with two sailing boats. My mother handed my father a cup of tea.

'I've got something odd to tell you,' she began. I pricked up my ears but continued to paint, hoping they would forget I was there.

'What's that, sweetheart?'

'Rhoda Downer, the schoolteacher, was here earlier. She told me that when she was saying her prayers, she felt very clearly that God was saying to her, 'Don't worry. It's going to be all right.' But the really strange thing is this, Phil. Before she came, exactly the same thing had happened to me too. I felt absolutely clearly, as if a voice had spoken, that God was saying just that. Don't worry. It's all under control.'

I put down my paintbrush. This was something new.

'Then I've got something even stranger to say to you,' said my father, taking a sip of tea. 'I've been all round the village again, and one person after another told me 'has Hi say my prayers, it jus' seem God say to me 'Don' worry,' he say. 'Don' worry.''

They sat in silence for a little while. I stared at them, trying to read their faces. My father put his cup down.

'It does seem very clear that God is speaking to some of us, individually. Nobody has got together with anybody else to concoct this story, out of wishful thinking. The fact that it's happening to people separately, but they are all getting the same message, is remarkable and we must take it seriously.'

My mother refilled his cup. 'I agree, Phil. But it's a risk.'

'I suppose it is. But then I wonder – what is the meaning of a risk, with God? Haven't I been saying that our Lord was with his friends in an open boat on the sea? It follows that he is with them in those boats.' He paused, and took a gulp of tea. Then he went on 'Just to complicate matters, I saw the administrator. He says we're going to have to call off the search. There's no more hope.'

'Well he's wrong,' said Mum vigorously. 'There is hope. God has told us. That's that.'

My father sat a little longer, then said 'I'd better go and get ready for tonight's prayer service.'

I went on painting, thinking about what they'd just said. How could people be really sure that God was speaking? But it sounded as if they all were. And if they were right, then the administrator was wrong.

'There's only one way to find out,' I said, washing my paintbrush and contemplating my painting.

'Find out what?' said my mother, who was busy now with some mending.

'Find out if you and Miss Downer and the islanders and everyone is right. And the administrator is wrong. Which is, if the lost boats come back.'

'Well,' said my mother, biting off the thread. 'We must just trust God.'

We had early tea again, and once more followed Dad up to a full church. As I sat down and took Christy from my mother, I glanced round. There was something different. The atmosphere was not the same as the previous evening. I started turning the pages of a board book for Christy, and when the hymn started, I stood him up on the pew so he was surrounded by people singing. He liked this. He stopped fidgeting and stared intently at the people behind us, and I kept an arm round him, just in case he should take off.

Again at sermon time my father stood informally on the chancel steps instead of in the pulpit. All rustling and movement stopped, but tonight there was something different about the way people were listening. Almost as if they were waiting for something, but this time they knew what they were waiting for.

Dad always spoke simply, and his face never betrayed his feelings. He always seemed calm, even when I knew he was upset or worried or pleased or excited. I could not see any difference in him.

'I thought I would have some very sad news for you this evening,' he began. 'As you will know by now, the administrator thinks that we should call off the search. There is very little hope after so long.'

There was a stricken silence. Or was it? As I reached up to Christy to sit him down on the pew, I caught sight of the islanders' faces in the dim light of the Tilley lamps hanging from their hooks overhead. This time there were no tears, only a curious calm.

'However,' said Dad, 'I'm not going to tell you that.'

I watched him as he made his characteristic, unconscious gesture of pulling the sleeves of his surplice down to his wrists, and smoothing them. 'Instead, I'm going to tell you something surprising. As I've been going round the village today, one by one many of you have told me the same thing. In your prayers, God has said to you 'don't worry.'

I'd like you to know that when I got home from visiting, my wife said exactly the same thing to me, and so did someone else from the station. Therefore, I believe that God is speaking to us in a special way. Instead of telling you that there's no hope, I'm going to say the exact opposite. God is saying to us 'there is hope. Don't worry. It's going to be all right.'

The atmosphere round me changed, as if there were invisible colours swirling around us. I didn't know what it meant, but I could feel it. When I got into bed that night, I realised I was excited. Something would happen.

Very early the next morning there was noise and stirring throughout our house. 'Quick,' said my father, coming fully-dressed into our room, 'get ready. The met officer's seen one of the boats.'

Mikey and I, barely awake, tumbled out of bed. 'Where? Where?' we shrieked.

'He was making his dawn observations, and saw a sail – that's all I know.' Dad rushed out of the

155

house, running across the pebbles and through the garden gate, up the side of the valley. Scrambling into our clothes any old how, I dragged on Ba's dress over her head and taking her by the hand, we raced past Mum who was bundling Christy into a ganzey.

The red rays of the rising sun were only just coming over the shoulder of the mountain, but people were flowing like a stream out of the station, down from the village, all going past our house in the same direction to the edge of the cliffs. We ran to join those who were already standing behind the barbed wire fence, and there we all saw it. A single boat on the horizon, the brightness of the rising sun filling its white sails with rose light, heading in our direction.

I turned to Mum. 'It looks like an angel boat,' I said.

Her voice choked. 'I think it is,' she said. 'It is an angel boat.'

I knew what she meant.

Two hours later *Tristania* radioed that she had sighted the other boat, the one with Jennifer Rogers. We all rushed down to Big Beach, as the boats landed and the exhausted crews were helped ashore. They looked haggard and sunburnt, but had been strong enough to take down their own sail and mast when they reached the *Tristania*. They had gone aboard and the fishing ship had taken their boat in tow and brought them home.

Their families were there, weeping and hugging them, pressing food and drink on them, knowing how little they had had over the four days. I heard the administrator shouting 'No! Don't give them any food! And only very small sips of water, or you'll make them really ill!'

Ned Green, Eldon Lavarello, Joseph Glass, George Glass, Bernard Repetto and Jennifer were taken to the hospital to join Big Harby Glass, Victor Rogers, Morris Green and Chrissie Swain, the crew of the boat we had seen sailing towards us that morning. They all stayed there for a few days but I heard the grownups remarking on how quickly they all recovered.

A week later Jennifer was back at school. When she came into our class we had written 'WELCOME BACK JENNIFER' in coloured chalk on the board. When she opened her desk, she found a present of some wool and knitting needles from us, her classmates.

She didn't say anything at all, but we knew all right. By now we all knew. During the four days' ordeal, 'little Jennifer' as the crew called her had been up to her knees in sea water as she baled out the boat while the men rowed. She had eaten raw mollymawk, and been given the last glass of drinking water. The sea had been so rough and the wind so strong that it drove them away from the island in an east-nor-east direction, towards Africa, making it impossible to turn the boat round.

On Monday afternoon they had all said a prayer together, and the wind had dropped at last. They hoisted sail and turned to steer south-west. That night they had seen the lights of a ship, but had no torch to signal. Instead, they had a hunting rifle which they had taken to Nightingale to kill sea birds, and so they fired three shots. The ship never saw them. The rifle came in useful the following

157

day, when a shark, sensing their helplessness, started circling their boat and came in so close they could see his teeth. They shot it.

Eighteen hours later, on Tuesday afternoon, they finally sighted the island like a bump on the horizon. It was the day and time that people on Tristan had become convinced that God was telling them that they were going to be all right. The crew kept the mast between two big stars. Little Jennifer said that they was like the wise men, steering by the star.

Little Jennifer, said the men, was niver skeered.

'I still cannot even hear the sound of that hymn, Eternal Father strong to save, without welling up,' says Mike.

'For an atheist, that's quite an admission!'

'I don't think it's anything to do with faith.'

'What then?'

'I remember visiting more recently the Penlee disaster monument, and I stood there and cried and cried.'

We're on the phone to each other, and I wait. For all his cerebral approach to life, Mike could always be very emotional.

'Is it to do with the power of the sea and the helplessness of humans?' I ask after a moment.

'I think so. And that hymn. Eternal Father, strong ... 'his voice over the phone chokes, and he pauses, then tries again. This time he doesn't even get through the word Father.

'Can't do it'.   His voice catches again. 'Something to do with the tune.'

'It's a bit dirge-like.'

'It's those words – 'oh hear us when we cry to thee' – it's complete helplessness ... 'his voice breaks up. Eventually he adds 'It's that sense of utter helplessness.'

I understand, but what strikes me most is the extraordinary experience of the islanders – that complete reassurance, independently of each other, that 'has Hi say my prayers, it jus' seem God say to me 'Don' worry,' he say. 'Don' worry.''

And they were right.

11. GOING ON LEAVE

Mikey and I, wrapped in our windjammers, watched the orange helicopter flying towards us over the sea from HMS Protector. Over the past week we had all helped to pack, ready for going back to England for our leave. Our parents, with Christy and Ba, had already gone ahead to the ship. It was so exciting to be flying without them, on our own, accompanied by one of the officers.

HMS Protector

Mikey started jumping up and down as the helicopter began to descend, its blades whirring. He always did when he was excited. We stood well back with the officer as the helicopter touched down, the whirling rotors creating a wind that blew the grass flat in a wide circle. The door in the side opened.

'Keep your heads down,' ordered our officer. 'You don't want them chopped off by those blades – your parents might have something to say!'

We ducked down obediently until we were next to the body of the helicopter, safely out of the reach of the rotors, and climbed aboard.

We took off, watching through the window as the plateau diminished in size below us, the houses growing smaller and smaller like monopoly pieces. The helicopter climbed steeply until we were over the peak of the island. We had never been up here, 6,000 feet above sea level, and we looked down curiously, seeing the lake in the crater cradled by the peak.

'That's because it's an extinct volcano,' I shouted to Mikey over the noise, knowledgably.

'I know,' he shouted back, not liking to be told things by me.

Below us on the other side of the island in the lee where it was calmer, the Protector was at anchor on a steely sea marked with long lazy lines of swell. We flew lower over the ship until we could make out Daddy, waving to us from the deck. The helicopter slowed, and hovered, and touched down feet away from where he was standing. This time the engine was switched off, the rotors slowed and then stopped. We climbed out.

'By Jove!' said Daddy. 'What a lot of noise and wind! Did you enjoy that?'

We were adjusting to the movement of the deck, automatically spreading our feet apart.

'Rather!' I said.

'Come and see where you're going to sleep,' he said. 'I think you might find it rather exciting.'

161

He took us down into the ship to the cabin where he and my mother would sleep with the two younger ones.

'There's nowhere for us here,' observed Mikey after a quick glance round.

'Aha,' said Dad, 'that's a surprise. Follow me.'

Agog, we followed him down another companionway to what seemed like the bottom of the ship. Here, nearer the engines, the crew had rigged up two hammocks and two camp beds. Partrick and Gargie, the administrator's children, were already there. They were coming with us to Cape Town because it was the end of their father's tour on Tristan.

'The hammocks are for the boys,' said our father. 'The camp beds are for the girls.'

'Oh!' I said angrily. 'Why do the boys get the hammocks? I want one!'

'That's the fact of the matter,' he said firmly. 'This is what the captain has decided and we all have to do what he wants.'

'Why are girls not allowed? It's not fair!' I said, my pleasure at the helicopter ride and the prospect of a voyage alloyed by this discovery. 'Boys are always allowed to do more things than girls!' I looked him in the eye. 'It really isn't fair, you know,' I told him.

'Never mind, just make the best of it,' he said. 'And because you're rather a long way from us, you'll have a Royal Marine called Barry. He'll sleep outside your door, so if you need anything in the night he'll look after you. The Captain says Barry has children at home so he's a good person to do that.'

162

A real Royal Marine to guard us! I decided the hammock wasn't worth fighting for.

At bedtime that night Partrick was a pain, leaping from his hammock to Mikey's and then back again, announcing 'I'm now going to transfer to this hammock. Now I'll transfer to this ...'

I could see Mikey was getting fed up. 'Stop it, Patrick. I want to settle down,' he said. Partrick took no notice.

'And now I'm transferring back again,' he continued, leaping on to Mikey's hammock. Mikey gave him a shove. 'I told you, stop it!'

I could see that this might end in a scrap. I was the eldest and thought I should stop it, but I didn't know how. I was relieved when the door opened and their father stood there.

'Patrick! What are you doing? You should have gone to sleep a long time ago! Settle down at once.'

And Partrick did.

Five days later we docked in Simonstown in South Africa, and went down the gangplank to be greeted by Bishop Roy Cowdry. We climbed into his car and en route to his house, he stopped and bought us all ice creams. We had not had proper ices for three years and we licked them gratefully. Bishop Roy shared his home with his sister Freda. It was a big white building on the top of a hill, with stoeps (veranda and balcony) on the ground and first floors.

Uncle Roy and Aunty Freda, as they told us to call them, had furnished a room for our parents and had borrowed a huge white cot for Christy. We all dumped our cases on the floor. It was immensely hot: although Tristan was on the same latitude with Cape Town its exposed position meant it was never too hot. Here, we were already sweating. I went through the bedroom doors which opened on to the stoep and leaned over the parapet. It overlooked the garden with its damp green grass, bordered with orange canna lilies.

At bedtime I had an idea. 'Can we sleep on the stoep?' I asked my mother. 'It's so much cooler out there.'

She hesitated, looking at me. It would be crowded for us all to sleep in the same room, and the heat was making her uncomfortable too.

'I don't see why not,' she said. 'It looks safe enough. You and Michael can both sleep out there on the floor. But you have to behave and not do anything silly.'

'Hurray! I promise you, we will be ever so good – won't we Mikey?'

He nodded, and started to drag his mattress out through the folding doors. This was a wonderful treat.

We only wore pants at bedtime. It was too hot to put on nightclothes. We had a sheet to put over us, but I kicked it off. I lay on my back, looking up at the blackness of the night sky, watching the dancing pinpoints of the stars. I would like to sleep outside for ever.

While we were there my father had business to do in Cape Town. In-between times, we were taken out to visit some of the acquaintances and friends we had made three years ago. When we weren't doing that, our favourite pastime was to run through the hose which was always playing on the lawn. It was the best way to cool down.

Ten days later we boarded a Dutch cruise liner, the Waterman, for our fortnight's voyage home.

When we got to England, we found that the mission had not organised any accommodation for us, and friends in Lancashire who had said they would be able to provide something, failed to do so. We went first to Bushey, to the relatives who had put us up before we went to Tristan three years previously. With eleven people in the house, wash days meant mounds of sheets as well as clothes heaped up on the scullery floor, waiting for their turn in my aunt's twin tub. My mother and she took it in turns to wash, rinse, mangle, and carry outside to the lines where I helped to peg it all out. When we weren't helping, we played clock golf with our cousins which was set out in their garden, trying to improve our score.

Next to Barrow in Furness to stay with my mother's parents. Grandad had had another heart attack and I knew my mother was very worried. He was a short, lean man with white hair and moustache and an irascible personality. We children were fascinated to watch him taking snuff, and then sneezing very loudly. Although my mother didn't want us to 'bother' him, Mikey soon discovered that Grandad, who had been a Royal Engineer, spent hours in the garage tinkering with his pride and joy, a black Singer SM 1500. Mikey loved finding out how things worked and he and Grandad soon developed an affinity, working on the car together to decarbonise the engine.

We were taken for outings in Grandad's car, a high treat: we played in the garden and climbed the apple tree, while my mother spent hours talking to Grannie, the two of them on chairs in the kitchen. I always thought how alike they were. They would both hunch over in the same way, Grannie twisting her hands endlessly in her lap, and they talked with the same anxious inflection in their voices.

At Land's End while on leave

From there, a very long journey to Cornwall in the car Grandad lent us, to visit Grandma and Grandpa at St Sithney Vicarage near Helston, all along roads with hairpin bends which we had never seen before. Grandma with her white hair in a bun and still with a soft Irish lilt to her voice from her Tipperary childhood, and Grandpa with his twinkling blue eyes, always full of jokes and tricks and stories. The big vicarage and garden were ideal for us: we ran around noisily and played, fed the ducks on the pond, collected eggs and went to the beach. My mother had had my hair cut into a fringe for the first time, and Grandpa, always so warm and approving, didn't really like it. 'I would like to see your brow,' he said. I didn't know what to answer. If I disagreed, it would be thought rude. It seemed a pointless thing to say, but I didn't like being disapproved of through no fault of my own.

Then our cousins came to visit, and for the first time Daddy was able to catch up with his brother, Uncle Howard, who had left the Royal Air Force to train for ordained ministry. They had long talks with Grandpa, also a priest, walking round and round the garden.

'Talking shop as usual,' sighed my mother, as we topped and tailed the black and red currants or the gooseberries outside in the sun, and helped Grandma produce enormous home-cooked meals for twelve people. One mealtime there were several puddings and Uncle Howard said

'Not much choice, then, Mum!'

Mikey and I looked at him: there was a twinkle in his eye and all the adults laughed. So it was a joke, then, I thought, as I put a large spoonful of golden syrup steamed pudding and custard into my mouth. But Mikey was puzzled.

'Why did Uncle say there wasn't much choice, when there was?' he asked Dad afterwards.

'It's called irony – you say the opposite of what you mean, and that's what makes it funny.'

But Mikey was about to come a cropper. The next day, again faced with a great array of puddings, he announced 'Not much choice here today, Grandma!'

Nobody laughed as Grandma dug her serving spoon into a rice pudding with a golden skin.

'Don't be rude, Michael,' said our mother, clearly embarrassed.

Mikey stared. 'But Daddy said yesterday it's called irony!'

Uncle Howard cocked a bushy eyebrow at his older brother. 'Out of the mouths of babes and sucklings!' he joked, and although I didn't fully understand, it was clear that he meant we children said things sometimes that were important.

Back in the car, and all the way north to Lancashire again, where my father had a three-week locum to take services for the priest of Haverthwaite so we could stay in the vicarage. Again it was a big house with plenty of room for us all, and friends and relations came to visit. Once there, my mother announced that we had to go to the local village school because we had missed so much, and it would be good for us.

Mikey and I immediately locked on to the Lancashire accent. When we got home from class we would make up sentences to include as many words in the local accent as possible. 'Will you help me loook for my boook?' we asked each other, stressing the long vowel. 'It is in the cup – board' we said as two words, screaming with laughter until we could hardly speak.

Out of school we played in the woods that backed on to the vicarage garden. We spent hours tracking each other through the trees and trying to get home without being caught. More cousins came to stay, including Naughty Lawrie, who knew more rude words than us. Thrilling. Shocking. And rather impressive.

When the locum came to an end we went south again to my mother's brother, then back to the long-suffering relatives in Bushey who once more put up our family prior to our return. Five months after our arrival in Southampton, we were there again, boarding the RSS *Shackleton*, a British Antarctic Survey ship which would take us all the way to Tristan. It would be a three-week voyage.

On the whole we loved being on the *Shackleton*. The crew enjoyed having a family on board and rigged up a swing on deck for us to use. Ba, now five, sat on it and while they rocked her to and fro she put her head on one side and closed her eyes. They smiled and told each other how sweet she was.

It was the first time I felt jealous of my sister. Why did they like her so much more than me? I started to show off, only to be scolded by Mum. I walked away to an empty part of the deck for a while, feeling confused and upset. I wanted to be liked as much as Ba. What would I have to do?

We were nearing the equator and it was very hot. The ship slowed down and, puzzled, I went back to the crew.

'What's happening?' I asked.

'Underwater peak,' said Mikey. 'It's never been charted so they need to mark it.' He was standing next to one of the FIDS, the young men who were part of the Falkland Islands Dependency Survey team. We really liked the FIDS – they took time to explain things to us.

The *Shackleton* began to turn a circle.

'Why are we going round?' I asked them.

'We're conducting a sonar survey to pinpoint exactly where the peak is,' said one of them, dressed like all the men just in a pair of shorts.

'I don't know what sonar means.'

'I do,' said Mikey smugly, which annoyed me because I wanted to hear it from the FIDS. 'It means that you send out sound waves and they make a pattern which shows where the peak is.'

I glanced at one of the FIDS and he nodded. 'That's right. And when we know the precise reference, we'll mark it with a buoy. We can't have other ships scratching their bottoms on a hidden mountain!'

Mikey laughed and I smiled uncertainly. It sounded a bit rude to me.

The ship's engines were cut. For the first time for several days there was unaccustomed quiet: just us on one ship with the open sea all round us as far as the horizon. We seemed very small and vulnerable in that huge blue world. The purposeful hustle and bustle of the FIDS and the crew was reassuring.

I joined some of the sailors, hanging over the railing as we waited for the work to be done. One, and then two of them stripped to their underpants and dived into the sea, swimming away from the ship in an attempt to cool down. I stared, wondering how they had so much courage. Miles of water below them. Why weren't they scared?

Then the first mate in his uniform of white shirt, shorts and socks came sliding down the companionway and ran to the railing.

'Come back!' he shouted. 'Come back immediately! There are barracuda about!'

I watched, my heart in my mouth, as the men in the sea swam furiously back to the ship and were hauled aboard unceremoniously. It was a huge relief when they were both safely aboard. That had all been so dangerous.

Once the yellow buoy was in place over the undersea mountain the engines restarted and we moved off again. As we went, flying fish leapt aboard and we caught one, holding out its wings for the camera before throwing it back in the water. Then, as if to underline what the first mate had said, a large black shape swam smoothly alongside us.

I hung over the railing while Dad rapidly wound the key on the cine camera.

171

'Quick!' I said to him. 'Is that barracuda?'

'No,' said a FID, 'it's a shark.'

The cook was on deck, watching with the rest of us. He disappeared and came back a moment later with a lump of bacon and an S hook, which he started to bend into the shape of a fish hook. Then he fastened it to a piece of rope, baited it with the bacon and threw it over the side.

The dark shape, moving with oily ease, glided to the surface and in a moment the bacon was gone. I drew back. I might be safe but I didn't want to be so near. That effortless, silent ferocity was frightening.

We sailed on, one hot day moving into the next as we drew near the equator. One day we were finishing lunch in the mess when one of the FIDS came in and said to another 'Go on deck! You can see the equator!'

The other FID barely raised his eyes from his book. 'Not bothered, seen it before.'

I ignored them. I had picked up my own book and was keen to get back to the story. Then I heard Mikey say to Ba 'come on – let's go and look!'

They disappeared before I could say that there would be nothing to see, and went back to my book. It was too hot to run after them.

A few minutes later they were back.

'Did you see it?' asked a FID, with a faint smile around his mouth.

'I saw it,' reported Mikey. 'It's like a faint hazy line all across the sea in front of us.'

'I saw it too,' Ba informed us.

I looked up and opened my mouth, but the FID was ahead of me.

'I'm afraid you can't see anything,' he said. He looked slightly ashamed. 'You can't actually see the equator. It's a notional line round the middle of the planet, equidistant from the poles.'

Mikey's blue eyes gazed at him, assessing him. The FID said 'Sorry, old thing.'

Mikey turned away. I looked reproachfully at the FID: that had not been fair, trying to fool a little boy.

Maybe they wanted to make it up to us, because that evening Dad said 'if you like, you can stay up late tonight. The FIDS say they will take you up on deck and tell you all about the stars.'

'How late?'

'About eleven o' clock, I think.'

Mikey jumped, turning as he did so, and made an imaginary gun with his hand.

'Bang bang!' he yelled. That meant he was not just pleased, but ecstatic.

So that evening, full of excitement, we went up on deck. One of the FIDS, the one with the shaggy beard, told us to lie down on the tipping deck and look up into the sky. The stars were pin sharp and brilliantly clear. He sat down next to us and I watched his arm as he swept it between us and the sky, indicating with a pointing finger the long wide trace of starlight which was called the Milky Way, as if somebody had spilled a bottle of milk. Then he pointed out Orion, and Cassiopeia's chair, the Great and Little Bears and other constellations, and finally the Plough. He showed us how we could use the Plough to find the pole star, and explained how it had always helped sailors find their way on voyages.

173

It was magical. When we returned to our lessons on Tristan, astronomy became one of our favourites. I can still pick out Orion and the stars in his belt and sword, and every time it takes me back to that heaving wooden deck, still warm with the tropical sun of the day, and the balmy night, and the stars, and the FID with the shaggy beard pointing up into the sky.

'I think you should dump this chapter,' says Mike's voice on the phone.

'Why?'

'Not really. Nothing much happens. It's just a series of events.'

'But it's what happens still, to so many missionary families − going 'home', which isn't really a home, not having a house of their own, travelling about all the time. We've done it ourselves, when we were mission partners in Nigeria. It's a very insecure situation, and usually we are only too glad to get back to the country we know and love. Ba was very unsettled in England, and only recovered when she got back to what she called 'my island'."

'Hmph,' he says.

I've left it in.

12. THINKING ABOUT GOD

When we returned to Tristan life rapidly returned to normal. My father resumed church services and teaching the seniors at the school, and both he and Mum were often out visiting the islanders, especially those who were ill.

One day my mother said 'Take these potatoes to Granny Mary,' and handed me a basket with a cloth over the top. 'She's in bed poorly and I said I'd send her some.'

I took them and started off on the path that led up to the village to Granny Mary's house. I had to pass the church on the way, which was always open. I hesitated, then went in.

St Mary's church

It was very quiet inside, the sort of quietness that churches have, where the prayers have soaked into the walls. I walked up the aisle and into the sanctuary, took a quick look round to make sure there was nobody watching, then laid the basket on the altar.

'Thank you for these potatoes,' I whispered. Then, embarrassed by myself, I took the basket, left the church and went on.

After my visit I decided to walk across the village and go the long way home. It had been a day of sunshine and showers, and just now the heavy grey clouds hanging over the sea were parting. I paused and stared. The sun was shining from behind the clouds, throwing long straight dancing rays that fell onto the moving steely sea and turned it silver. Something in my spirit soared out to meet them until I was part of that strange beauty. Maybe angels come and go up and down those rays, I thought. They look like heavenly pathways.

That night I got out my 'Saints for Six o'Clock' book again, which I read and re-read. I was appalled at the suffering of some of those old martyrs. What would it have been like, to be St Catherine and broken on a wheel? I was deeply impressed with her courage, but also distracted trying to work out how you got broken on a wheel. My imagination set off down a road that was too dark for my liking.

It was the same with St Laurence who was roasted on a grill, because he would not give up being a Christian. How could he just say 'I'm done enough on one side, turn me over now' to his tormentors, in the middle of the most shocking agony?

I couldn't imagine myself going through such torments. That must mean I didn't love God as much as they did. I felt guilty, but comforted myself by hoping that I would never have to make that decision. Then I wondered if I was being cowardly.

God had been part of our lives ever since I could remember. Our meals were set by the rhythm of my father's daily services. We always prayed by our bedside at night. God was the context in which we lived, sometimes puzzling, but always there. Somehow, I wanted more, I wanted God to become more real.

I put down my book, and made up my mind. After supper that night I tackled my father.

'Daddy, you know some of the schoolchildren are going to be confirmed next year?' I started.

My father looked up from reading the Cape Argus. 'That's right. Bishop Cowdry is going to come out from Capetown to do it.'

'Well,' I said cautiously, 'can I be confirmed too?'

I could see that I had all his attention now. 'I don't think so, darling. You're only nine, and people have to be at least eleven.'

'Oh please Daddy,' I said. 'I've been thinking about it for simply ages. I say my prayers and go to church and I really badly want to take Communion.'

'We'll see,' he said.

'You're always seeing! And usually that means you're not going to do anything, you just want me to keep quiet!'

He looked at me, amusement crinkling the corners of his green eyes. 'Well, this time I do mean I'll see. I'll talk to Mummy, and if she agrees, I'll radio the Bishop, and see what he says.'

I flung myself on him and hugged him. 'Daddy, you're supersonic!'

'By Jove!' he said, hugging me back. 'Where did you get a word like that?'

'Dan Dare,' I said succinctly, and went to bed happy.

My parents did discuss it. 'She's always been interested, Phil,' said my mother. 'Don't you remember the time she brought her doll to you in church to be baptised, when we were still in Downham? She must have been about three.'

My father chuckled. 'I was right in the middle of a baptism too,' he remembered. 'I told her I'd do it later!'

My mother smiled in response. 'I was watching her kneeling next to you in church on Sunday, when you were taking the intercessions.' I always picked up my kneeler and took it into the aisle, setting it down next to Dad while he prayed. 'That child wants to be a priest. It's a pity she's a girl in a way. She's an absolute pocket version of you. We should have called her Philippa.'

'Do you think so?' said my father.

'She's even got your nose.'

'Poor child!'

Radio messages went back and forth between Tristan and Capetown, between Bishop Roy and my father. One day he came into the house holding a cable in his hand.

'Gilly, I've got some supersonic news for you.'

'What is it?' I asked curiously, trying to read his face, which looked both pleased and mysterious.

'Here's a cable from Bishop Roy. He says that because you want to be confirmed so badly, he's willing to do it.'

'Even more supersonic!' I yelled, throwing myself at him and hugging him round the waist, then jigging up and down round the dining room.

'What's supersonic?' enquired Mikey, coming in at that point with his latest toy boat in his hand.

'I'm getting confirmed I'm getting confirmed I'm getting confirmed' I sang.

'Hmph,' he snorted. 'I thought it was going to be something interesting.'

That summer I joined the other youngsters, four girls and six boys, for confirmation classes with my father. We sat round the table in our kitchen in the evening. Some of us were on the built-in cupboards which my parents had had made all along one wall. They had sliding doors with holes in, and inside there was shelving for the citrus fruit which came out occasionally by ship from Capetown. Sometimes we kicked our heels against those doors, making a hollow sound, and were ticked off by my father.

As the light waned, he lit a pressure lamp and hung it from a hook in the ceiling. The light deepened the shadows and contours of our faces as we bent over our Catechism.

Q. What are the sacraments?

A. The sacraments are outward and visible signs of inward and spiritual grace, given by Christ as sure and certain means by which we receive that grace.

My father made sure we understood what we were reading. It wasn't enough to learn it all by heart, which we did anyway. With simple examples and images, he connected the meaning of the catechism to our everyday lives on the island and with the convolutions of our human hearts. I had no trouble accepting that we were all sinners. It was obvious to me from the behaviour of others and from what I knew of my own thoughts and attitudes. And I was glad and relieved that God had sent Jesus to sort it all out.

My parents gave me books for preparing myself before taking Holy Communion, one of which was The Mass our Sacrifice from the Church of the Province of South Africa. It was wonderful that all the drawings were of black priests and black servers and black angels and black people. Strangely, Jesus was white, although one drawing showed him as a black child with Joseph, who was also black. I puzzled about that, but it was obvious that God loved all of us equally, whatever our colour.

Another book had a drawing which fascinated me. There was one of a boy in front of a bowl of water and underneath it said 'Bill washes his hands.'

The next drawing showed him jumping up and down on his sister's doll, while she stood bawling in the background. The words said 'Bill loses his temper.'

The final picture was the one I went back to most often. It showed Bill with white hands but a dark heart, and the caption read 'Bill needs his heart clean as well as his hands.'

It made perfect sense.

Right at the end of January, a month after I had turned ten, Bishop Roy arrived on the HMS Lynx for the confirmation. We were all delighted to see him – my parents because they had become very good friends during their enforced stay in Capetown, we children because he was fun, and especially me because he had said yes. The cut-down bridesmaid's dress, now 3 years old but still fitting me, was once more pressed into service. On my head I wore a white confirmation veil.

The evening service of 1 February 1959 was a Solemn Evensong, a major celebration in more ways than one. For a start it was the patronal festival of our church, dedicated to St Mary the Virgin. Then the Governor of St Helena was there, having also arrived on the Lynx for a visit in his official capacity of the Queen's representative. First, we all stood in the crowded little church and sang the National Anthem. Then we girls in our white veils sat side by side in one of the front pews, and the boys, dressed in their smartest clothes, sat next to us.

At last it was time for the confirmation. The Bishop put his mitre on, sat down on the Bishop's chair and gave his crozier to one of the servers. Two by two we knelt on the hassocks in front of him. My father, standing near him, held a list with all the names of the confirmation candidates and the container of chrism oil. The Bishop dipped his finger in it, and I closed my eyes. I felt him trace the sign of the cross on my forehead and then place his hand on my head.

'Gillian, I sign thee with the sign of the Cross, and I lay my hand upon thee. Defend, O Lord, this thy Child with thy heavenly grace; that she may continue thine for ever; and daily increase in thy

Holy Spirit more and more, until she come unto thy everlasting kingdom. Amen.'

I listened avidly. This was for keeps. I was to belong to God for ever. I was to increase in the Holy Spirit until I died. It was for the whole of my life. I didn't know how I would be able to do it, but this wasn't the end. It was a beginning.

Bishop Roy was saying the same words to Minnie kneeling next to me. I opened my eyes, and saw the gold and red of the Bishop's cope framing his arms as they reached out to us, my father standing next to him in his white alb with the gold-embroidered stole around his neck, Mikey holding the boat of incense while Fardy Lars swung the censer. The fragrant white smoke swirled around us, filling the air in the church and spiralling up to the roof.

Minnie dug me in the ribs. The moment disappeared, I looked round quickly and realised we had to stand up and move away. It was the turn of the next two.

Afterwards, we all stood in a line together and the Bishop said to us 'Beloved, you have now, in the presence of God, who knows and sees all, ratified the promises of your Baptism, and have received of God the gift of his Holy Spirit. Wherefore I pronounce that you be admitted to receive the Communion of the Body and Blood of Christ. The Lord grant you his grace to consecrate your whole life and all your powers to his will and service in Christ Jesus.'

All my powers! My whole life. I wanted to give it all to him, although I wasn't sure quite how. Like the rest of the things I didn't understand, I put it away in trust.

The next morning, very early, it happened at last. I could take Communion for the first time. It was still dark in the little church at 5.30am, and I felt very quiet and peaceful inside. We girls were in our white veils again, only this time we sat with our families. A dish of candles was presented to the Bishop and he blessed them, then we were each given one. People's faces were pale in the dawn light seeping through the small windows. We each lit our neighbour's candle, the gold flames leaping from one to the next, their light flickering from one face to another. Holding the candles, we began the hymn for Candlemas, the presentation of Christ as a baby by his parents in the temple.

'Christ, whose glory fills the skies,
Christ the true, the only Light,
Sun of Righteousness, arise!
Triumph o'er the shades of night:
Dayspring from on high, be near;
Daystar, in my heart appear.'

I thought, if he appears in my heart, I will be ready to receive him in Communion.

When the time came, I felt confident. We had practised with Daddy, and anyway, I had been watching it all my life. I went up with Mummy and my brothers and sister, and we knelt at the altar rail together. I watched my mother receive the bread, then I made the sign of the cross and held out my own hands, one cupped inside the other. For the first time, the wafer was placed on them and did not pass me by. Then came the silver chalice, which my father tilted very slightly so that I had the merest sip of the sharp, sweet liquid. I wasn't sure I liked it, but it didn't matter. This was it. I waited until the person on my left had received it, then I got up and followed my mother back to our seats.

Did I feel any different? I felt very special. I knew something important had happened. But I had expected to feel more, which worried me. I didn't know what I should be feeling, but in the end I decided that was less important than what I knew to be true.

To this day, the feast of Candlemas transports me back to the still, dark hush of our island church, with the candlelight moving warmly on hands and faces in the early morning gloom.

'My confirmation was a negative experience,' says Mike.

'Why?' I don't remember his confirmation at all.

'It was years later, when we'd returned to England and were living in Crawley near Winchester. It came my turn for Confirmation. I knew that Dad was insistent that people took this seriously and attended the preparatory classes etc. However, I went into hospital soon after they started and missed most of them. When the Confirmation came up I assumed I would not be doing it. When I found out I was to be confirmed I protested that I hadn't been properly prepared. I still remember what Mum said – "Don't worry,

184

Daddy will tell you afterwards." I even remember her tone of voice. But Dad never did.'

'How old were you? Did you go away to St John's School at that point? Because you were a boarder, so that would explain it.'

'It was certainly one of the first times I started to question Christianity. If this 'serious' thing could be so easily put aside for the sake of what? To stop people asking why the Rector's son was not taking Communion?'

'I'm afraid that's entirely possible. Mum was so terrified of what people thought, and the needling remarks they would make to her at the church door.'

'I remember the ceremony in Winchester cathedral – a sense of 'What am I doing here?" Mike adds.

'So for you it was much more about 'if other people don't think it's that important, then neither do I'?' I ask.

'I think so.'

'It was entirely different for me. I did go through a serious time of doubt in my teens. It was the sixties, and the teaching staff at school told us constantly that we should take nothing for granted, that we should not accept things other people said to us, that we should test everything and experience everything and find out for ourselves.'

'That was very sixties.'

'I remember coming home from sixth form one day. We'd had a PPE lesson and we'd all been asked how many of us believed in God? Very few people did. Most people did not put up their hands. I put mine up, but very hesitantly, because I wasn't at all sure any more.'

'And yet in Crawley we went to church three times a Sunday – Communion at eight am, Matins at eleven when were were in the choir and we both rang the bells, and again at six-thirty Evensong.'

'I helped Mum in the afternoon with Sunday School too for a time. I'm not sure how I ever found time to do my homework.'

'What happened?'

'I remember walking back to the car park in Winchester with Dad after a Good Friday procession of witness through the city, and almost crying, and saying 'I can see it's all real for you, Dad, but it isn't real to me.'

'So what was important for you was that inward sense of truth.'

'Very much so. And when I went up to university, I still wasn't sure. I'm certain that, if I had not come to a living faith in Christ at that point, I would have experimented with drugs. It was very much part of the scene, and nobody knew the terrible health risks which have emerged since then.'

'In other words, you could say that your faith changed the course of your life at that point?'

'Even now I thank God for that. I've come to the conclusion that somehow, although my confirmation was not able to provide me with the personal reality of God that I longed for, it did provide a framework like a log cabin, something that held me steady while I was questioning.'

13. HUP THE WILLAGE

It was Miriam and Aaron's wedding day. There hadn't been many weddings for a few years. It wasn't easy starting married life, because the would-be groom needed to build his own house, which he did with the help of the other men in the village. They cut by hand huge blocks of brown stone or 'tuff' from the mountain, just behind Jenny's Bog, and brought them back to the site in bullock carts where they were squared off and used for the gable ends. Once the walls were built with small windows and a stable-style wooden door, it was time to thatch the roof with flax.

The men slashed swathes of New Zealand flax from the numerous hedges that grew around the buildings as protection from the constant gales and storms.

'They're thatching the new house today, children,' said my father. He had slung the cine camera in its case over his shoulder. 'I'm going to watch and get some film. Do you want to come?'

We didn't bother to put our shoes on. We ran around with bare feet like most of the other children. We hopped and skipped beside him uphill to the village and the half-finished house.

Dad got out the cine camera, had a word with the men, then wound the key and began to film. The flax was already in bundles, heaped up on the ground at the foot of the walls. The bundles were thrown up to the men on the roof.

'See how they're doing it?' asked Dad. 'There's one man inside, and one man outside. They share the thatching needle.'

It looked to me like a giant sewing job as I watched the men tying on the bundles with string or nelly yarn. The islanders were quiet people, and there were just the odd murmurs: 'nip' for when the string was gripped to stop it slipping: 'haul' for when the string was pulled through from the thatcher outside to the one inside: 'up' when the string was tight enough and then a call 'bundle' for the next one.

'How many rows of bundles do they need?' Mikey asked Dad. He went up to the working men and asked, taking Mikey with him. Six each side, they said. And then turf for the ridge.

Once the roof was done, the little cottage, usually only two rooms, would be lined throughout with wood and painted. It was easier to get wood then, not like earlier days when the only wood available was from shipwrecks, and single girls joked about praying 'Lord, please send me a shipwreck so I can get married.' If however that tragedy happened, the islanders earned a name for themselves by rescuing the passengers and looking after them, at their own expense, until a ship could be found to take them off the island. With vastly improved navigation aids shipwrecks were rare, but some ships were still uneasy about getting too close into the island.

Island houses, thatched with and surrounded by flax

I thought about the coming wedding, and what I'd heard my parents say. It was some years since Aaron had taken himself off to Miriam's house where she lived with her parents. One evening he had walked in quietly, greeted the parents and sat down with the family. The wood fire flickered. The pressure lamp hissed gently. Miriam's mother made him tea. Her father smoked a pipe with him.

Miriam said nothing and occupied herself with her knitting.

Indeed, nothing was said throughout the evening, but by the time Aaron got up to go, it was understood that he was 'coatin'' (courting) Miriam. She knitted him some socks, and a ganzey for Christmas. He went on coming to the house, month after month, sitting in the room with them all, and saying little. There were no demonstrations of affection – the islanders did not approve of such things in public.

For the wedding, Aaron borrowed a suit and tie, and Miriam a wedding dress from the doctor's wife on the station. My father took the wedding to which everyone was invited. Then it was time for Big Heaps.

The whole island took part in these, which marked not only weddings and baptisms but also first, twenty-first and fortieth birthdays. We children, dressed in our best – my gold-spotted cut-down bridesmaid's dress was pressed into service again – followed the crowd from the church to Miriam's parents' house.

The people from the station were ushered inside first and we found a long table, made by the island men, laid for the meal with benches on either side. It was a sunny day so there was a smaller table outside with a lot of bottles on it. I didn't take much notice of these, not realising that they were full of whisky and gin and other spirits which could be bought duty-free on the island. We children were given Oros or Lemos, South African versions of orange and lemon squash.

Mikey and I scrambled onto the benches, our parents close by, other expatriates on our table. The food was brought in.

It was always the same, and we fell on the roast stuffed mutton first which we loved, heaping up our plates with mashed, boiled and roast potatoes. Then it was time for the puddings. We could have spotted dick, a suety recipe with dried fruit, put in the corner of a flour bag, tied up with string and boiled until it was cooked and served with custard: or we could have what my mother called Tristan tart. This was a pastry case filled with custard and cooled until it was set. Then tins of condensed milk were boiled for several hours until the contents turned to a soft toffee consistency, which was spread over the top of the tart.

Mikey was asked what he would like. 'May I have both?' he said politely, but Mummy tut-tutted and told him off. 'Michael, of course you can't – don't be greedy! You've just had a huge first course!'

We were fed up, but now our mother had noticed, we had to accept what she said. If she hadn't noticed and only Miriam's mother had heard, we knew she would have given us both. As it was, we opted for our favourite, Tristan tart, which was now sitting on the table. I kept an eye on it as we ate. Hopefully there might be a bit left over and I could have seconds.

We never liked to tell our mother, but we preferred the island tart to hers. She made egg custard instead of ordinary because she said it was better for us, but it didn't have the rich sweetness of the island version.

Tucking into my pudding, I was half-listening to the chatter of the station adults around me. It was all boring as usual, and I was wondering when it would be polite to thank the hostess, climb off my bench and go out to play. The woman opposite me was a young South African wife with long black hair which she wore swept into a knot at the nape of her neck. I knew she had just had a baby because we'd been to visit several times, and I usually went with my mother on such occasions because I loved babies and often had a chance to hold them.

Suddenly Mrs A began to cry and shout. Her eyes grew unfocused and her face twisted. 'My baby!' she wept. 'Where's my baby? The devil's got my baby!'

I stared, fascinated. What was going on? She looked as if she wasn't in control of herself. Her cutlery clattered on to her plate and she half-turned away from the table, the people next to her hastily making room.

'Get the doctor at once,' said my father quietly.

Was she ill? What did she mean? Did the devil really have her baby? Surely not. Then why did she think that he had? Her distorted features and her screaming and wailing was frightening and intriguing at the same time. What sort of illness did she have? What would the doctor do?

My mother and some of the other wives helped her off her bench, talking soothingly to her, assuring her that the devil did not have her baby, and to come with them outside into the fresh air.

The rest of us sat there in silence for a moment. I could tell the adults were all shocked by what had taken place. Then they went back to their meal, talking in quieter voices than before.

My mother came back inside, and beckoned us. 'Come on children. It's time to go home.'

'But I want some more pudding,' Mikey said.

'You've had plenty. Now come along with me,' and she bustled us firmly outside. I realised that she was trying to get us away from an adult world which had suddenly shown hitherto-unknown cracks, like the gulches running down the mountain and across our plateau. We stopped arguing and followed her reluctantly.

Later, back at home, I asked her the question uppermost in my mind.

'Why did she start doing that crying and shouting? Why did she say the devil had her baby? Is that true?'

My mother looked at me. 'Of course it's not true, darling. She just isn't very well. She started believing that because she's not well.'

'What's wrong with her?'

'Well, I'm not sure. But some mothers do get something like this sometimes when they've had a baby.'

'Did you get it?'

'No. I've always been perfectly fine.'

I was not a demonstrative child, but I went up to her and put my arms round her neck.

'I hope you'll always be fine for ever and ever, Mummy.'

She gave me a kiss. 'Don't worry about it. The doctor will give her something to help her stop worrying. I'm sure she'll get better soon.'

I learnt later that Mrs A was to be shipped back to South Africa on the next available ship.

Life was good, life was happy on the island for us. But it was no romantic idyll.

My mother was very aware of the undercurrents in the lives of the expatriates on the station, who came from the 'houtside worl'' as the islanders put it. But she was wise and very tactful and managed to steer clear of gossip. As she and Dad did constant visiting 'hup the willage' she became very fond of the island women, and they of her.

She and I did a lot together. When we returned from our leave in England, we discovered that the island school, although it would continue as a church school, had reverted to the Colonial Office and so she no longer had to teach, as she had done previously. With so much help in the house and with Christy, she had time to spend with me. Some of this was teaching us our lessons now that we were being home-schooled, but there was leisure time left over when she taught me to bake, or made new dresses for my dolls.

She sometimes took me with her when she went visiting, especially when she went to Alice and Sidney. Sidney was one of Christy's fardies, and he and Alice were really good friends of our whole family. Their daughter Trina taught the infants in school, and as Mum was a professional nursery school teacher she was soon supporting and guiding Trina in her work. We saw Trina's younger sister, Pamela, quite often when she came to our house to practise hymns for Sunday on our piano. They had another daughter, Valerie, who had gone to England with a previous school mistress, and my parents created a piece of cine film of the family to show to Valerie next time we returned home.

We loved visiting Sidney and Alice. While my mother sat and talked, I would take Sidney's collie dog Captain outside and throw a stick for him. I had been terrified of dogs since one had knocked me down when I was two, but playing with good-natured Captain was a breakthrough for me.

Today though Sidney was out with Captain, but Alice was busy. All the ganzeys, socks and hats on the island were knitted by the women, using fleece sheared from island sheep, and then washed clean. It had then to be carded and spun, and today Alice was hosting the carders and spinners.

I watched them for a while as they dabbed wool on the carder, then briskly brushed it to and fro into fluffy sausages, which they put into piles ready for the spinner. It looked like something I could do. Could I try?

Alice showed me how to attach the wool on the sharp points of the carder, very quickly and evenly, and she set the carder ready on my lap. Then I took the other one and brushed it up and down on top, to make the skein of wool fat and soft. It was much more difficult than it looked. I got too much wool the first few times and then the carders stuck together. If I brushed too lightly it didn't separate the fibres enough. Alice let me practise for a while, but in the end she took over again. She had a lot to get through, and clearly, I did not have a natural aptitude.

It was a sunny day and the carders were sitting in a row on chairs outside in the garden. They were surrounded by a low drystone wall and gladioli and wallflowers were growing in the flower beds. Mum sat down with them to chat, so I wandered to the other end of the garden where Mary had set up her spinning wheel away from everyone else because she needed a lot of room. She sent the wheel round, attaching a sausage of carded wool to the thread she had already created. Magically, as her fingers and hands danced, she drew out the thread longer and longer to the full length of her arm.

I so much wanted to have a go. How difficult would it be? I thought I'd start with something easy.

Spinning (not Mary)

'Can I spin the wheel for you?' I asked. Mary paused and looked at me. She was a fair-haired woman with blue eyes, which just now looked doubtful. But she said 'Sure you can, my li'l girl'. I waited until she had picked up the next fat fluffy roll and started to attach it to the thread she'd already made, then I spun the wheel.

I spun it too fast. She caught the wheel with her left hand, the thread breaking in her right as she did so. She didn't say anything. She didn't even seem cross. She just said 'y'all done spin the wheel too fas' and set it going again, this time pulling out the thread without mishap.

When she had finished that one, she stopped again and looked at me. 'Y'all wanna spin?'

'Yes please,' I said eagerly, and took the spun thread in my hand, attaching the roll of wool as I had seen her do. I spun the wheel.

The thread broke immediately. Mary mended it for me and I tried again. This time the thread grew longer, but I could see it was all uneven. 'Y'all mus' practise!' she laughed at me, and took over the wheel again. I watched her some more, trying to discover the secret of it. She had practised for years and years, since she was little. That must be it.

The weather was not always this sunny. The island was exposed to unpredictable South Atlantic gales, and everything – the fishing, the potatoes, the visits of big ships – depended entirely on the weather, as they do to this day. We soon adapted, learning to resign ourselves to the huge disappointment when ships with our mail had to take it back to Capetown because it was too stormy for the boats to go out to them and unload; or when things we had ordered and needed did not arrive in time. We made the most of the sunny days, going down to the beach or playing in the garden with a paddling pool.

On just such a day Mikey and I were up on top of the hut. It had been given to us by the previous schoolmaster who had built it out of wood, with a corrugated metal roof. As Daddy already had a shed for his stuff, at one end of our veranda, he only kept a few tools in this hut and we were able to use it for play.

It was such a warm day and we were only in underpants, because we'd been given permission to paint the hut and Mummy had said she didn't want paint on our clothes. We'd done the outside walls and we'd climbed up on the roof to make a start on that. Mikey began at one end, and I at the other.

I wasn't sure that Mikey's paint was going on evenly, and such things bothered me.

'Stop a minute,' I told him.

'Why?'

'I don't think you're putting it on properly.'

'Course I am,' he said scornfully. 'Think you know more than me?'

I regarded his work. 'Look. Can't you see? You've hardly covered the metal here, but it's really thick over there.'

'Oh leave me alone,' he said crossly.

We painted on in silence for a little while, and then, paintbrush in one hand and can of paint in the other, I took a step back to see how it was looking.

And found myself falling. I had walked back into thin air. I landed on the ground with a crash and a jolt. My paint flew everywhere and I started to scream.

I dimly remember Mikey peering over the roof at me, then scrambling quickly to the ground. He

198

jumped the rest of the steps down to the house and raced through the front door, but by that time my father, who had been working in his study, had heard the commotion and come running out and up the steps.

As he reached me my mother came out of the house and called 'What's going on?' By that time my father was bending over me, asking me where it hurt, while I was gasping and crying and sobbing as much with shock as with pain. Having established that I had apparently not broken anything, he picked me up in his arms and took me down the steps into the house. I was put into their bed, and my mother got in next to me. I lay there sniffing and tearful.

'What on earth were you doing?' she asked.

I gulped, my breath coming in spurts. 'I wasn't doing anything naughty! I stepped backwards and fell off and it was awful,' I wept.

'Well that was a bit silly,' she said vigorously. 'That will teach you to be more careful.'

I felt this was deeply unfair. 'I was being careful! I just didn't realise ...' and I cried again.

She hugged me. 'Never mind. You don't seem to have broken anything. It all could have been a lot worse.' She got up and fetched me an aspirin and a drink of water. Not long afterwards I dropped off to sleep.

When I woke up I felt fine, and that evening, after the geyser had been lit for hot water, she put both Mikey and me into the bath and gave us scrubbing brushes. 'Try and get some of that paint off yourselves,' she said. 'That should take your mind off things!'

We scrubbed and scrubbed. Mikey got fed up before me, and still with paint on him climbed out of the bath and dried himself.

'Mummy will make you get back in and get it all off,' I warned.

'No she won't. I'm going to put on my pyjamas so she won't see.'

Mikey could be duplicitous.

That was early in the year in the summer. By August it was mid-winter, which was never very cold, but when the South Atlantic gales blew in full force. Shipping rarely came to Tristan during the winter.

One Sunday night I woke and listened. The wind was howling round the house. I discovered that our mother had been into the bedroom during the night and closed our window, which was nearly always open. Even with it shut, I could hear the swishing and creaking of the flax hedges just outside, the moaning as the wind tried to find its way in under the corrugated iron roof, and the wild noise of a crashing sea.

I loved being inside when there was a storm. I went contentedly back to sleep.

The next morning Harriet arrived, looking windblown. As she took off her headscarf and tidied her hair, she said she had met Daddy going up to church for early Mattins. 'I done say to Faather, the willage hall roof it done blow clean away,' she said to my mother as they busied themselves getting breakfast.

I combed my hair in the kitchen, listening. The village hall was barely finished. After Prince Philip had laid the foundation stone more than a year previously, teams of island men had worked together to build the walls, put up the girders, and fasten the corrugated iron on for the roof. It sounded as if all that work had been wasted.

My father returned two hours later.

'What's going on?' asked my mother. 'Where have you been all this time? I've been worried to death about you. Harriet says the hall roof has blown off.'

'It looks as if a giant's finger has ripped through silver foil,' said Dad. 'It's in ribbons, and it's dangerous, because pieces keep coming off and blowing around. Then I walked through the village – some houses have had their thatch torn off and there are gaping holes in their roofs. Nobody seems too upset though.'

'I'm very surprised,' said my mother, putting a plate of lightly-fried bacon and eggs in front of him. 'Most people would think it was terrible if their roof was destroyed.'

Harriet brought in the freshly-baked bread that she and my mother made weekly between them. 'Y'all know, you'se can't truss Haugust,' she said.

'That's what I'm told,' said Dad, tucking in, hungry after a busy time without breakfast. 'On my way home I called in to look at the school building. The roof over the veranda was lifting in the wind and I had to find some tools and four-inch nails to secure it. I think it will hold now.'

He looked at Mikey and me, standing there agog at hearing all this news. 'I've got a surprise for you two,' he said.

'What?' we chorused.

'Your hut's disappeared.'

'Disappeared!' I exclaimed.

'How?' asked Mikey.

'The wind must have picked it up and blown it clean over the flax hedge. It's smashed to smithereens – there are bits of wood and metal all over the garden and outside in the gulch and on top of the cliff. I've never seen anything like it.'

'What about your tools, Daddy?' asked Mikey anxiously, as he sometimes borrowed them to make things out of wood and he had left them in the shed.

'Fortunately I found the plane and the set square and the hand drill on the ground near the house.'

'Phew! That was lucky.' Mikey was relieved.

As my father finished his cup of coffee there was a shout on the veranda. We went out to find Hedbit (Edward), one of the Scouts, for whom Dad was the leader.

'Faather, the scout dinghy it done blow clean away,' he said.

'Right,' said Dad, wiping his mouth on his napkin. 'Let's go and see.'

'Can we come?' I asked.

'No.'

'Ohh! Why not?' we chorused, aggrieved.

'It's dangerous. Dave Watt, the met man, is recording gusts of 150 miles an hour. It could pick you up and blow you over the cliff into the sea.'

We digested this. 'How does he know?' demanded Mikey.

'He's a met man. It's his job to measure wind speed and things like that.'

'I want to go out in it!' I said grumpily.

'It's not safe. You will do as you're told,' announced Dad in his not-to-be-argued-with voice. I pouted, and stamped off, and when he had gone Mikey and I crept out on the veranda. We ducked down low so we would not be seen by our mother through the windows, and surveyed the flax hedges, all higher than our bungalow, flattening in the gale. Pieces of wood and metal were flying through the air. We did not dare go any further.

Meanwhile my father and Hedbit had gone up to the village and collected Hedbit's father and others. Bent almost double against the wind, together they found the scout dinghy 500 yards from its original place. They pulled it under a bank and lashed it down more firmly.

After lunch we begged and pleaded to be allowed out in the gale. At first our parents kept saying no, but as the day wore on they relented.

'Only if you do exactly as I tell you,' ordered Dad. 'You'll come with me and we'll hold hands at all times.'

'We promise!' we said, jumping up and down.

'I come too,' announced Ba.

'No, you're too little,' I said, jealous of our privilege.

'I not too little,' she argued, but my mother said 'you're not going out, Ba. Stay in with Mummy and you can do some painting.'

It was not cold. I put a ganzey on over my yellow cotton canteen dress, and then we set out with my father, holding his hands tightly. We crossed the garden to the gate: our house, being at the head of a small valley and surrounded by the tall flax hedges, was the most sheltered on the island and so at first the wind did not seem so strong. It was only as we climbed up the side of the valley and reached the top that the full force caught us. We gasped, tightened our hold on Dad's hands and put our heads and shoulders down into the wind. It battered us and bowled us along and was utterly exhilarating as we struggled down to the cliff edge and looked over with great caution. The grey Atlantic rollers roared over the beach where we normally had picnics. The sea covered it entirely, throwing spray high up against the 200-foot cliff so that we could taste the salt on our lips. We watched in awe as vast waves as big as houses tossed and swirled and crashed against the rocks, ran out foaming white, gathered themselves together and hurled themselves with renewed strength against the cliffs on which we stood. We found ourselves in the middle of an alien world, and for the first time I realised that the screaming gale that battered us and the raging waves were destructive powers utterly indifferent to the lives of weak and puny humans like us. We crouched down on the ground, huddled together for safety.

It was three days before the wind dropped sufficiently for repairs to be done. My father went out with the island men to collect up the corrugated metal pieces of the hall roof, some of which they found half a mile away. They took them back to the hall and stored them inside, and the islanders, phlegmatic as ever, began to patch the roof as best they could. That day several people could be seen on different roofs around the settlement, also patching where the flax had been ripped out and the turf ridges of their houses destroyed.   Once they had finished their own repairs, they came in relays to help repair the hall.

'How are they getting on?' my mother asked when my father returned.

'There's been an accident – Louis Swain fell off the roof.'

'Oh no,' exclaimed my mother. 'Is he all right?'

I felt for Louis. I knew what it was like to fall off a roof.

'Some of us took him to the hospital where Doctor Roshan checked him over thoroughly. He doesn't appear to have broken anything. Remarkable, considering that he fell on concrete!'

I was impressed. I had only fallen on grass and that had been bad enough.

'What's more,' added my father, on his way into his study, 'he got off the hospital bed and walked home. They make 'em tough here!'

'OK,' I say to Mikey, staving off what I suspect will be his comment, 'so nothing much exciting happens in this chapter, except for the storm – and even storms are not that big a deal on Tristan because they have so many of them and they deal with them in the same down to earth way they always have. It's about the way we lived. The way they lived.'

'We took it for granted,' he agrees. 'People were different from us and did things differently from us, but that was normal life.'

'I think that living on Tristan, and living in South Africa even for those few months, meant that we

205

absorbed from a very young age that life was full of interesting people living in interesting ways. There was never any suggestion that they were 'less' than us. Simply different'.

'We've said before that our parents' apparent attitude in treating everyone the same was something we soaked up unconsciously,' he muses. 'But as I've got older, I realise more and more how many people identify that others are 'different' somehow, and they allow that to become a barrier.'

'Particularly so with the rise of social media, which give platforms to people wanting to express negative and unpleasant opinions about those whom they consider 'other'.'

Mikey thinks, then says 'It seems to be so prevalent that people find one thing they don't like about the 'other' person, and they use that as a reason to dismiss the whole person.'

'I know. I find it very concerning.'

'One of the reasons I enjoyed travelling so much when I was younger' Mikey goes on, 'was the enjoyment of meeting people with different backgrounds and opinions. Although they were 'other' than me that made them more interesting, not less.'

'I'm sure now that our childhood experiences had a big influence on my calling to be a mission partner – that sense of wanting to live in another culture because it was fascinating. They fostered my curiosity – why do people do this? How do they think? – and an enjoyment of discovering what was different.'

'It was always interesting. Always something new to learn.'

'Our biggest problem was when we came home to England. Suddenly everyone was more like us. It drained the cultural colour out of our lives.'

'I remember those first few months after we came home for good,' Mikey says reminiscently. 'I was out in the garden and I was bored rigid. I had never been bored on Tristan. There was always something calling to me to explore and discover.'

'I was bored too, for years, while I was at grammar school.'

'No wonder we both ended up going abroad again.'

14. OUT WITH THE GANG

When we had been on leave in the Lake District, my parents had taken us to a large rambling house in a sunny garden in Ambleside. It was the headquarters of the Parents' National Educational Union. They had decided that on our return to the island, they would teach us at home. This would help to ensure that we were level-pegging with children of our own age, when we finally left Tristan and were in England for good.

So we no longer went up the steps and the long wooden corridor to school on Tristan. Instead, our mornings were spent with our parents on a range of subjects that were not available there. We did English and history and picture study with Mummy, and Daddy taught us mathematics and geography and religious education. We had nature study, when to my delight I was given an exercise book in which the lined pages were interleaved with blank ones. Carefully, I drew the wildlife that was around us: rockhopper penguins, mollymawks, starchies, and the unique flightless rail which was only found on Nightingale Island in the whole world. My mother had loved this subject when she was at school, and proved much better at drawing than I would ever be.

With our mother in the garden

I was enchanted with the new subjects. I had never heard of Picture Study before, and I spent a long time, poring over the beautiful soft pinks of Fra Angelico's Annunciation, the exquisite golds of the angel's wings and halo, the gentle folding of the arms echoed in Mary, the quiet courtyard with its delicate pillars. I could feel its beauty soaking into me until it was like a physical longing. I wanted to be part of it. In the same way I tasted Botticelli, Michelangelo, da Vinci, Goya and others, teaching me to appreciate art in a way that was to stay with me always.

Then there were the Legends of Greece and Rome which I studied, along with Greek texts in

English. I picked up the dark blue hard-backed book, tooled with a gold border on the cover, and opened it. Inside the front cover was a bookplate with multi-coloured floral patterns surrounding the letter A, awarded to my mother on reaching first place in Form II at Crosslands convent school in 1934. I spread open the pages with care: some of them had been rough-cut, and they were interleaved with engravings. I read and re-read the legends, following Atalanta in her tunic, stopping to pick up the golden apples as she ran. Why did she do that? Was she greedy? Didn't she see it was a trick?

I watched Icarus spiralling up into the sky on his wax and feather wings. He ignored his father until the wax melted and he fell to his death. So you should obey your parents because they usually know best, I thought, or at least, they knew more than you. It was stupid of Icarus, but maybe he found it just too exciting.

Then I wondered why Echo fell in love with a man who was only interested in his own reflection. My imagination, always vivid, roamed free in these new worlds.

I began to learn French and Latin, and excelled in English, reading and writing. I had nobody to compare myself with apart from Mikey, and he didn't count really because he was younger. The only annoyance was that he continued to be much better at arithmetic than me, fast and accurate, ready with the answers to mental sums while I was still slowly working them out.

Arithmetic became a literal as well as a metaphorical pain. On my father's fortieth birthday I was standing next to him in his newly-built study. His desk was under the window and we could look out on the green valley and fields in front of our house, which ran down to the sea beyond. He was trying to explain decimals to me. I concentrated hard, but just couldn't get it. I would follow his explanation so far, and then there was a blank wall in my mind with no door.

Dad was a patient man and tried explaining the concept from different angles. In the end even he lost heart.

'Do you see that telegraph pole out there?' he said in exasperation.

'Yes,' I said miserably, well aware that I was falling short and therefore in some way doing wrong.

'Well it's as plain as that!' he exclaimed.

My heart sank. I didn't know what else to do. How could I understand something that I couldn't understand? But I had to try. He gave me some exercises and sent me away to do them.

I sat at the table in the dining room under the front window, pummelling my brain, willing it to find a way through the maze that presented itself to me. I went over and over the explanations, trying to apply them to the exercises.

After a while I began to notice a pain in my abdomen. At first I ignored it, but it got worse. I decided that I needed a walk and some fresh air, so I went out and strolled along the path behind the house. The pain didn't go away.

I went back indoors and found my mother.

'I've got an awful pain in my tummy.'

'Perhaps you've eaten something. Do you feel sick?'

'N-no,' I said, considering it, 'it just hurts.'

'I'll give you some aspirin and you can go and lie down.'

I did. The pain got worse and worse until it hurt whichever way I lay, and I began to vomit. Normally the islanders gave a big party on a fortieth birthday, but I could hear my father in the next room explaining to a visitor why it wasn't going to be possible that day.

Over the next few hours the pain steadily increased until I was crying with it. Finally, my parents sent for Dr Master, a Pakistani Parsee woman who had been a consultant surgeon in Nottingham and had spent much of her working life in mission hospitals. She came and prodded me gently and I doubled up and groaned.

'I can see that hurts,' she said in her calm and sensible way. I nodded – it was all I could do.

'I think she's got appendicitis,' she said to my parents, and then to me, 'We'll have to give you a little operation.'

I nodded again. I didn't care what happened so long as the agonising pain was taken away.

I was taken over to the island's four-bedded hospital, five minutes away. The doctor and Nurse McKinley scrubbed up and put me on the table, and I looked at them with the masks over their faces above me: the doctor's calm brown ones, the businesslike blue of Sister. I remembered having anaesthetic when I had had my teeth out in Cape Town, so it was no surprise when they put a mask over my face and told me to breathe deeply while

212

Mr Simpson, the agricultural officer, tended the machine behind my head. Red and brown circles swirled before my eyes and I began to feel sick again, and that was all.

When I came round, I was in bed in the hospital. I opened my eyes to see Sister sitting on a chair knitting quietly.

'You're awake – good,' she said.

'What's happened?' I croaked.

'The doctor's taken out your appendix. You've got a strap on you.'

I lay there fuzzily trying to work out what she meant by a strap. It was some hours later that I discovered she meant a dressing.

That night my mother slept in the other bed in the ward. Next day neither the doctor nor the nurse were there, and Mummy came over to the bed.

'You need to get up, Gilly,' she said. 'It's important to start moving around.'

I could hardly move with the acute tenderness in my side.

'I can't,' I said. 'It hurts too much.'

'You must,' she said. 'It's better to do it with me now, than to be made to do it later with Sister.'

I wept and pleaded, but my mother was firm. I must get up. Eventually, gritting my teeth, I found that if I rolled on my good side and pushed myself up with my hands, it was painfully possible to sit up. Getting out of bed was agony and I cried again at how much it hurt, but my normally soft-hearted mother helped me take a few steps across the room and then back to the bed, where I thankfully lay down.

'There you are, you see!' she said. 'You've been very brave. Now we can tell Doctor and Sister that you've been out of bed, and they won't make you do it today.'

A day or so later my mother helped me put on my pink dressing-gown, and my father lifted me up in his arms and carried me home from the hospital and into my own bed.

The pulling of the stitches whenever I moved continued to be painful, but ten days later the doctor and nurse came to remove them. Nurse pulled fast at the dressing and I gasped because it hurt, but then I was able to see the place where the doctor had cut me, low down on my right-hand side. There was a red five-inch scar, the edges held together with black thread.

'This will sting a bit,' said Doctor matter-of-factly. I felt she expected me to be brave again, so I tensed and waited. And it did, but finally the last stitch was out and Sister was cleaning the wound.

'That looks very healthy,' she said.

After they had gone my mother came in to see me.

'Doctor says that if she hadn't operated when she did, your appendix would have burst,' she said. 'It was already swollen. She's kept it in a jar for you – do you want to see it?'

I was very curious and nodded. My mother went and fetched it. I stared at it: it was like a bloated slug.

'Ugh! It's foul.'

'Well, you can see where it's swollen at one end, almost halfway along.'

214

I took another look. I already knew that the operation had been necessary, but now I could see why.

'Doctor didn't have any suitable suture,' she remarked, sitting down on my bed.

'What's that?'

'It's special catgut that surgeons use to sew up people. So we had to use some sewing thread from the island canteen instead. That's why the stitches were black.'

It didn't occur to me that this was anything out of the ordinary.

Our lives changed in more ways than one, with the advent of home schooling. We were not in the island school every day and so keeping up our friendships wasn't as easy as before. On our return to Tristan I discovered that a South African family had arrived with a daughter called Sandy, the same age as me, and we spent a lot of time together. Then she went back to Capetown with her family, and my mother worried about my lack of friendships.

'She sometimes plays with the boys on the station,' says her letter to her mother, 'but then she gets teased and she minds, and won't do it any more. I do feel anxious that she doesn't have more friends, but she seems quite happy.'

I was happy, because I had discovered writing. I put together a play, and nagged my friends to take part in it. They were none too pleased, being mainly boys who loathed dressing up; but their parents came to my play and clapped politely. It was too much trouble persuading the boys to do more acting, and I was in a quandary: I had read all there was available to read, including all of Enid Blyton's 'Adventure' books, which I loved, and I had run out of books. To make up for it I decided that I would write a story myself, the sort of tale I enjoyed reading most. I spent hours in my room, covering sheets of lined quarto paper as I took two children through their adventures along a river to a hidden valley where they rescued an enslaved people.

Then there were Saturdays.

Mikey and I rushed into the kitchen to see our mother. Peter and Jonathan, the other members of our gang, had just arrived.

'Please can we go and play?'

'Have you made your beds?'

'Yes' we chorused.

'Have you brushed your hair and tidied your rooms?'

'Yes!' we said again, Mikey beginning to hop up and down in frustration.

'All right then. Just be careful.'

She always said that. We ran outside before she could think of any more duties for us.

Peter, Jon, Mikey and I had formed a gang. We modelled ourselves on the Enid Blyton's Secret Seven: we had a secret motto and password, and we met in the empty chicken house in their garden. We even had a flag: Peter had broken off a tall flax stick from the hedges of flax which were everywhere, and we planted it firmly in the ground outside the hut and made a jolly roger to fly from the top.

Our name was a secret. Peter and Jon's mother was very good with her sewing machine, and made us badges with TSS stitched in red on a brown background.

Mikey and I took ours home to lunch.

'Guess what it means!' I challenged our parents. Dad took a shot at it. 'Tristan Secret Society'?'

'No!' we yelled. 'Guess again!

But they got it wrong every time, and we were sworn to secrecy. We would never tell that our gang was called The Spooky Spooks.

This Saturday we began with a quick conference. We would go down to the beach and first, we would go fishing. Peter and Jon already had a line with a hook on the end – not a real hook, because our parents all regarded that as too dangerous. It was frighteningly easy to catch a finger in a real fish hook and then not be able to remove it. A nail, hammered into a hook shape, was what we used instead.

'Hang on a minute then,' said Mikey. 'I'll go and get our fishing tackle.' He doubled back up the garden and into the shed at the end of the veranda, and emerged with a length of string and another bent nail. I went back into the kitchen, where Harriet was busy lighting the gas for the oven.

'Hish y'all got some bait?' I asked her. She hesitated – it wasn't part of her job to decide what meat to give away. My mother came in and said 'What do you want?'

'We're going fishing. Can we have some bait?'

'I should think so. Now let me see ... 'She went to the meatsafe and opened the wire cage door. There was some cold mutton in there on a plate: she took it out, cut off a piece and wrapped it in some greaseproof paper.

'Thanks Mummy!' I shouted and ran off again outside. The others were getting impatient.

'Come on' said Jon, and we went down our valley to Garden Gate beach.

The cliff was broken down at the point where the valley ran into the beach and it was easy to descend. Peter was the first to reach the black sand and he stopped short.

'What is that?' he pointed.

By this time we could all see it, a huge white structure which was sectioned, taller than we were. We ran up to it.

'It's the backbone of a whale,' Peter said. We ran our hands over the huge arches of bone and walked all round it.

'Makes you realise what a massive creature the whale must be,' I said.

'And this is only a small bit of it,' Mikey observed.

Jon stepped back and considered it. 'I don't think we can climb it – it's too smooth and slippery.'

We left the whale bones and began to walk towards Little Beach, the kelp surrounding us with its strong, salty smell and the sandhoppers in it fleeing at our approach. We could get to the beach along the shore under the cliffs when the tide was out, although the sand disappeared between Garden Gate and Little Beach and we would have to pick our way over the black boulders. On our way we decided to climb the low grey rocks that humped out into the ocean beyond, forming pools of different shapes and sizes. We stopped on a long rock at one side of a deep pool.

'This looks a good place for fishing,' said Jon.

We considered it. We had become much more adept at knowing what sort of rockpool might harbour fish. 'Yes – it's nice and deep.'

We squatted down on the rock, baited our bent nails, attached them to the strings and lowered them into the water. We watched the movement of the sea running in and out of the pool, the black sand lying at the bottom of the clear Atlantic water, the brown and green kelp moving forward and back with the tide. In places it was so thick that it hid the bottom, and although it was the most likely place to find fish, none of us wanted to keep catching kelp on our hooks.

Nothing happened for a long time. Jon kept pulling his line up to have a look, and we argued about how long to leave the bait in the water before we checked it. He and Mikey got fed up with waiting.

'I'm going round the other side of the pool,' decided Mikey. 'I might have better luck over there.' He and Jon climbed back to the sand and then out on the rocks at the other side.

Peter and I stayed put, discussing the reason for finding no fish, and working out how long we would have before the tide came in and closed off our access to Little Beach. I pulled out my hook to check it, found nothing, and lowered it into the water again.

'I'm going to take a look and see if there's any fish hiding under this rock,' I told Peter.

'Good idea,' he said. 'It has quite a big shelf on it below the surface.'

I crouched on the edge, hanging out over the water, trying to look under the shelf.

At that moment a long red tentacle lashed upwards, attaching itself to the rock within inches of my feet. I leapt back, my heart in my mouth. The tentacle withdrew, then flung itself upwards again, followed by a second one.

It was a catfish, what the islanders called octopus, and something which petrified me. A couple of years previously our family had all gone down to the beach to paddle and have a picnic. Mikey and I had our favourite rockpool which was the best for trying to swim. As I lay in the water I felt something wrap round my leg. Assuming it was a piece of kelp I looked down and was horrified to see a red octopus, its tentacles streaming, with one wrapped round my shin.

I have never been so terrified. I started to scream and struggle, catching a glimpse of Mikey moving very fast to the other side of the pool and climbing out rapidly on the rock. I looked down again – the most frightening things were the cold black eyes of the monster, but my kicking and fighting had dislodged the tentacle and, bursting into tears from sheer shock, I bolted out of the water.

Daddy had been taking off his socks preparatory to bringing Ba for a paddle, and as I splashed and screamed my way towards the safety of the beach, he came running to the water's edge with his socks still half on his feet.

'What's the matter?'

Mikey was dancing up and down and pointing and shouting and I was hysterical. As my father was trying to make sense of what we were saying the catfish swam not towards the ocean, but towards the beach. Mikey and I both shrieked a warning and as the creature found a channel between the rocks my father threw a well-aimed rock. The catfish shot out inky fluid and disappeared in to the neighbouring pool.

I sank down on the sand next to my mother, clinging to her, my heart pounding, sobbing into her shoulder.

'You're all right now,' she said soothingly. 'It's disappeared.'

'I am never going to swim in a pool again!' I wept. I scrubbed my eyes then and investigated my leg. I could see the marks of the suckers on the tentacles quite clearly.

These tentacles now, suddenly lashing up the rock with the clear intention of trying to get hold of us, were the stuff of my nightmares. Shocked, I yelled to the others 'There's a catfish and it's really cross!'

Peter had taken a cautious step backwards, but with the speedy arrival of Mikey and Jon we all scrambled down to a lower rock where we could have a better view.

There we all saw him, his protuberant, bulging black eyes glittering angrily, still flinging his tentacles upwards. Then he caught sight of us and immediately left his hiding place and flowed towards us.

'He's got it in for us,' exclaimed Peter, and we fled. I was seriously scared. This catfish knew we were there and hated us and wanted to get hold of us and drag us under water and drown us. We leapt inshore quickly from rock to rock until we reached the safety of the beach. No catfish could swim this far. I was relieved that the others weren't being brave either.

We rolled up our string and the boys put them into their pockets. We didn't want to go on carrying bait now fishing had lost its charm, so we threw it into a pool. We had another conference about how high the tide had come, and decided that there was still just time to reach Little Beach before the sea cut us off.

We scrambled over the rocks and boulders of the strand until we reached the stony bay which was Little Beach. Boats were often launched from here when the heavy swell and big rolling waves of Big Beach made launching difficult.

We stopped for another discussion.

'Nothing much happening here,' said Mikey, as we looked around.

'I know!' I said. 'Let's go all the way to Pigbite!'

'I've been there before,' boasted Jon. I looked at him. He was dark and stocky and mischievous, not always in a nice way, and I didn't like him as much as Peter his brother, who was quite different, being blonde and blue-eyed and very fond of reading, even more so than me.

'Well you don't have to come, know-all,' I said.

'Yeah,' said Mikey, equally annoyed. 'You can go back home if you want.'

'I didn't say I didn't want to come, now did I?' said Jon in an irritating superior way.

'Oh come on, stop arguing,' said Peter and set off with his long loping stride towards Big Beach.

I loved Big Beach with its long curve of black sand. I liked the hustle and bustle of the boats coming and going, of people working in and out of the canning factory. Several of the white long boats had been pulled up high on the beach and we walked round them, then left them behind us as we moved further away from the settlement. Big Beach marked its furthest point. After this, there wasn't much left of the plateau where we all lived. Now we were true explorers as we searched for the limit of our known world.

The dark sand became smoother, washed by the most recent tide, as yet untrodden. I turned and noticed how I walked more lightly than the boys with a much fainter impression from my feet. I noted it but said nothing – it was the sort of thing they would have scoffed at.

'There's the yacht!' said Peter and 'last one there's a molly' added Jon, starting to run. They were both fast runners and got there before me, but it didn't matter because the yacht, always there, was an enchanted thing.

Made of metal, it lay half-buried in the volcanic sand. We climbed over it, peered inside it, slid down the hull. It was mainly full of sand and we tried to scrape away enough of it to make a space inside for us to enter, but after a few minutes we realised it was futile.

'It's no good,' said Peter. 'It's packed tight and there's so much of it. We need a spade and it would take hours.'

Reluctantly we left the yacht, but as we walked on to Pigbite I wondered about it. How had it got there? It must have been shipwrecked. What had happened to the crew? Had they drowned or had they been rescued by the islanders? Every so often I looked back at it, so mysterious and romantic,

223

lying there beached and finished but full of its own secrets.

Big Beach ended when we reached tussocky dunes of softer, drier sand. This was Pigbite. We scrambled up the side, pulling on the long tussock fronds to help us although we knew that if we weren't careful it would cut our hands. Our feet and legs slipped and slid from under us, but we all reached the top and looked down the other side. It was a long slide of fine sand.

'Let's roll!' I exclaimed. We each chose a place to begin and lay down at the top, then rolled over and over to the bottom. It was wonderful fun. We climbed up and rolled down again and again, then stopped to discuss why it was so hard to roll in a straight line.

'I keep going crooked,' I said.

'It's because we lose our sense of direction when we're rolling,' said Peter, who knew things like that.

'I know!' announced Jon. 'Let's have a competition to find out who can roll the straightest!'

So we took it in turns, and the others judged, and in the end Jon won.

'Well done,' I said grudgingly, and we climbed back to the top. From there we could see the whole black sweep of Big Beach, the white factory in the distance, the grey cliffs behind it climbing to the green plateau.

'We've been here a long time,' observed Mikey. 'Look how far the tide's come in.'

'We won't be able to go back home via Little Beach now,' I said. 'The sea will be right up to the base of the cliff.'

'No, we're going to have to go up the path and along the top of the plateau,' decided Peter.

'I don't want to go home yet,' Mikey announced. 'Let's see where the spring is. I've always wanted to do that.'

'That's no problem,' said Peter. 'All we have to do is to follow the water pipe to its source.'

We all knew that the water for the island was piped from a fresh water stream as it came directly out of the mountain.

'Yes!' I said, jumping up, my interest renewed. 'And we can roll down here on to Big Beach!'

Covered in sand we set off, this time walking nearer the base of the mountain than the sea, along behind the factory and up the rough track beyond until we reached the uneven, boulder-strewn grass of the plateau. We struck off the track and made for the house nearest us which marked the end of the settlement, and quickly found the big water pipe as it emerged from the ground. We guessed its route and tracked it carefully, arguing whether we were getting it right.

'There it is!' said Peter. 'We finally made it.'

We scrambled up until we were against the sheer wall of the mountain base that soared above us. The islanders had captured the fresh water stream from the mountain into an underground tank, from which it was piped to all the houses. I put my ear against the rock wall, sure I could hear the rushing of the water inside.

'I can hear the water,' I announced.

'Let me have a go,' said Mikey, elbowing me out of the way. I stepped back carefully, turned and climbed down to the flatter ground at the bottom. Then I stared up at it. How mysterious of the water to run through the inside of the mountain – from where? Was there a spring inside that towering wall of rock where it all started? Or was there a stream from the peak, invisible from the plateau, which dived underground and emerged here?

'It's a clever idea,' I said to the others, 'capturing the water like that. I wonder where the source is?'

Even Peter didn't know.

Epilogue

I look at my brother now, thinking how differently we experienced Tristan.

'I wonder why it means so much to us still?' I speculate.

'I know what it means for me,' he responded. 'Being a boy between the ages of 5 and 10 on the island had a profound effect. Living amongst the islanders formed a subconscious image for me of what real men looked like. Real men drive ox-carts, go fishing, dig potatoes.'

'Whenever there was a crisis, nobody lost their heads or wasted their time weeping and wailing and wringing their hands. They all worked together to do whatever was necessary and they behaved as equals.'

'They were very grounded,' Mike agrees. 'For me that's linked to a feeling of security and reliability. As a result, I've always had a practical approach to life: DIY, grow my own food, not concerned with status. Consequently, like them, I've always been suspicious of authority and so not wanted to join it.'

'Isn't that a healthy thing?'

He pauses and looks out of the window, before turning on me that direct blue gaze which I've known since childhood.

'Not always. It's meant I haven't progressed in my careers.'

'You were too rebellious! How much do you mind?'

He pauses again, thinking.

'I probably minded more at the time than I do now. I'm at my most content fixing something practical and being in a boat. And making or mending something for someone is, for me, a giving of my deepest self.'

'That's profound.'

'I don't know about that. I get upset when people don't value the gift.'

Together we stare out of the window for a while. I have retired near the sea. I don't feel at home anywhere else.

'I find it harder to say what it means for me,' I meditate. 'There were things I didn't like, times I wasn't happy, times when I was lonely. But all the memory pictures flow together in my mind, still capable of creating in me an actual physical, gut feeling of adventure and excitement. It's there now, that bubble of expectation in my stomach. The mountain behind us ready to be explored. The sea in front of us stretching in an endless adventure to the rest of the world, ready for our boats. That never knowing what would happen next, which was our daily experience there and has made me restless ever since.'

He nods attentively.

'And the freedom,' I pursue. 'The sense that we could go anywhere, that there were always places to discover and new things to learn, that we didn't need to be watched and fussed over, that we could take off whenever we liked.'

We both sit there for a while in silence, our minds ranging back over the years to the black peak rising out of the South Atlantic Ocean and the green plateau which had been our home. That day when we climbed into a longboat for the last time, our luggage stacked around us, the salt spray in our faces as we rowed out to the ship we knew so well. Being on board the *Transvaal* was almost like home. It took us to Capetown, where we had three days; then we boarded the *Stirling Castle* for our final voyage to Southampton. We had no idea how much our life would change when we reached England, and not always for the better.

I still see them clearly in the garden of the little bungalow at the head of the grassy gulch that runs straight down to the sea. Four children are playing there, as they always will.

Printed in Great Britain
by Amazon